Recent Trends in Valuation

From Strategy to Value

Recent Trends in Valuation

From Strategy to Value

Edited by

Luc Keuleneer and Willem Verhoog

WILEY

Published 2003 John Wiley & Sons Ltd, The Atrium, Southern Gate, Chichester,
West Sussex PO19 8SQ, England
Telephone (+44) 1243 779777

Email (for orders and customer service enquiries): cs-books@wiley.co.uk
Visit our Home Page on www.wileyeurope.com or www.wiley.com

Other Wiley Editorial Offices

John Wiley & Sons Inc., 111 River Street, Hoboken, NJ 07030, USA

Jossey-Bass, 989 Market Street, San Francisco, CA 94103-1741, USA

Wiley-VCH Verlag GmbH, Boschstr. 12, D-69469 Weinheim, Germany

John Wiley & Sons Australia Ltd, 33 Park Road, Milton, Queensland 4064, Australia

John Wiley & Sons (Asia) Pte Ltd, 2 Clementi Loop #02-01, Jin Xing Distripark, Singapore 129809

John Wiley & Sons Canada Ltd, 22 Worcester Road, Etobicoke, Ontario, Canada M9W 1L1

Wiley also publishes its books in a variety of electronic formats. Some content that appears
in print may not be available in electronic books.

Library of Congress Cataloging-in-Publication Data
Recent trends in valuation : from strategy to value / edited by Luc Keuleneer and Willem Verhoog.
p. cm.
Includes bibliographical references and index.
ISBN 0-470-85029-9 (cased : alk. paper)
1. Corporations – Valuation.   2. Corporations – Finance.   3. Strategic planning.
4. Value. I. Keuleneer, Luc, 1959–   II. Verhoog, Willem, 1950–
HG4028.V3 R425 2003
658.15 – dc21

2002191089

British Library Cataloguing in Publication Data
A catalogue record for this book is available from the British Library

ISBN 0-470-85029-9

Project management by Originator, Gt Yarmouth, Norfolk (typeset in 10/12pt Utopia)
Printed and bound in Great Britain by TJ International Ltd, Padstow, Cornwall
This book is printed on acid-free paper responsibly manufactured from sustainable forestry
in which at least two trees are planted for each one used for paper production.

Contents

Preface   ix

About the editors   xi

**1   Introduction – strategic valuation: the relationship between   1
     strategy, valuation techniques and options**
     Luc Keuleneer and Willem Verhoog

     1.   Relationship between value-based management and   2
          valuation techniques
          1.1.   From strategy ...   2
          1.2.   ... to value   3

     2.   Option theory in the determination of value   4
     3.   Conclusion   6

**2   Valuation of companies: discounted cash flow, adjusted   7
     present value, decision-tree analysis and real options**
     Wouter De Maeseneire and Luc Keuleneer

     1.   Introduction   7

     2.   Discounted cash flow method   9
          2.1.   Description of the DCF method   9
          2.2.   Projected free operating cash flows   10
          2.3.   Essential for the WACC: the cost of equity   11
          2.4.   Importance of WACC in EVA$^®$ 16
          2.5.   Enterprise DCF versus equity DCF   17
          2.6.   Where can specific valuation parameters be found?   18

	2.7.	Critique of the DCF method	19
3.		Adjusted present value method	19
	3.1.	Description of the APV method	19
	3.2.	Critique of the APV method	21
	3.3.	Critique of DCF and APV	21
4.		Decision-tree analysis (DTA) and real options (RO)	21
	4.1.	Observations	21
	4.2.	Wrong interpretations of the DCF method (and APV method)	22
	4.3.	Real options and the analogy with financial options	23
	4.4.	When is the value of real options important?	24
	4.5.	What types of real options exist?	25
	4.6.	From decision-tree analysis (DTA) to real options	25
	4.7.	A few examples of real options	26
	4.8.	Equity as a call option on the firm's assets	31
	4.9.	Critique of the real option method	31
5.		Summary and Conclusions	32
		References	33

3. Valuation in practice — 35
Tom Copeland

1.		Introduction	35
2.		Discounted cash flow valuation	36
	2.1.	Introduction	36
	2.2.	Empirical tests of discounted cash flow	38
	2.3.	Discounted cash flow valuation of AOL	43
	2.4.	Discounted cash flow valuation of Amazon.com	49
3.		Expectations-based management	53
	3.1.	Company performance measurement	53
	3.2.	Expectations-based management: examples	56
	3.3.	Expectations and total shareholder return	63
	3.4.	Expectations-based management: an integrated framework	63
4.		Real options	64
	4.1.	Introduction	64
	4.2.	Coal lease valuation	69
	4.3.	Cancellable operating lease valuation	70
	4.4.	Consumer PC assembly business: exit decision	72
	4.5.	Plant construction: multiphase investment	75

4.6.   Natural resources: exploration and development   75
4.7.   Capital expenditures: a programme   78
4.8   Project analysis: a four-step process   80

Note by the editors   81

**4. Value-based management: control processes to create value   87
through integration**
Geert Scheipers, Anne Ameels, and Werner Bruggeman

1. Introduction   88

2. Value-based management   89
    2.1. Value-based management in perspective   89
    2.2. Defining value-based management (VBM)   89
    2.3. Why value-based management?   92
    2.4. The stakeholder approach versus the shareholder   93
          approach

3. Value-based performance metrics   94
    3.1. Introduction   94
    3.2. Listed perspective   95
    3.3. Not-listed perspective   97

4. Value-based management practices   103
    4.1. Introduction   103
    4.2. Value-based management in practice   103
    4.3. Value-based management as a practice   105

5. Conclusion   140

References   145

Index   151

Preface

In 2000, Wiley, together with VERA (Royal NIVRA's Committee for Continuing Professional Education), published a book entitled: *A Vision for the Future (Strategic Finance in the 21st Century)*. This was so well received – it has now, for instance, also been translated into Chinese and the Russian version will be published this year – that NIVRA/VERA and Wiley decided to publish a new book, dealing in greater depth with valuation techniques and their latest evolutions and trends, together with a discussion of these techniques within a more strategic framework.

After all, the term 'fair value' is becoming increasingly important, both for companies in general as well as for elements of their commercial operations, not only from a strategic perspective, but also from a financial and accounting perspective.

The result is this book *Recent Trends in Valuation: From Strategy to Value*. We have attempted to introduce in a conveniently structured and comprehensible manner recent trends in valuation. The express aim has been to adopt a middle course, in the sense that the book goes further than the traditional basic techniques relating to the various subjects. On the other hand, to improve the readability and understanding of the subjects, technical discussions that are irrelevant to day-to-day practice have been avoided as much as possible. NIVRA/VERA and Wiley are delighted to have been able to bring together a number of eminent authors to present the important themes appearing in this book to a wide reading public.

Willem Verhoog
Editor-in-chief

About the editors

Luc Keuleneer (1959)

Luc Keuleneer is a commercial engineer (Catholic University Leuven, 1981) and Master of Business Administration (Finance) (University of Chicago, 1983). He started his career as scientific assistant to the finance group of the Catholic University Leuven, and was later attached to the same university, commissioned by the National Fund for Scientific Research. He subsequently worked as adviser to the Cabinet of the Minister for Economic Affairs and Finance, as management attaché at Paribas Bank and as director at the Belgium Institute of Auditors. For a while he was also vice-chairman of the Executive Board of CGER-ASLK-Holding (now Federale Participatiemaatschappij) and Member of the Board and Audit Committee of CGER-ASLK Bank (now Fortis Bank). He has also been member of the board and member of the audit committee at Gimvindus, Werfinvest, Finindus, Sidinvest and 'L.B.-capital'. He has been a member of the privatisation committees of both the Belgium and Flemish government and was also a director at Deloitte & Touche Management Solutions NV, where he was jointly responsible for the Corporate Finance & Financial Services department.

At the moment, Luc Keuleneer is a director at KPMG in Brussels, where he is responsible for strategic financial services. He is a member of the Supervisory Board of Valkieser Communications BV in Hilversum (The Netherlands). In addition, he is a judge in the Brussels Court of Commerce.

He lectures at the Free University of Amsterdam and the University of the Netherlands Antilles as Full Professor of Financial Management and as visiting professor at the Ghent University, Vlerick Leuven Gent Management School and the Catholic University of Leuven. He also lectures corporate governance and value-based management as associate professor at the University of Maastricht and Royal NIVRA (Continuing Professional Education of *Registeraccountants*, VERA). He is a member of the VERA Board.

Luc Keuleneer has various publications in his name.

Willem Verhoog (1950)

Willem Verhoog has been Secretary-general of Royal NIVRA's Committee for the Continuing Professional Education of *Registeraccountants* (VERA) since 1 August 1976. Following the award of a teaching certificate at De Driestar in Gouda in 1971, he worked until 1974 as a teacher in Werkhoven and Alblasserdam/Kinderdijk. On the occasion of his 25-year NIVRA anniversary, he received a *liber amicorum* (with 25 contributions from professors) entitled 'How good is a timely word'. Verhoog is responsible for the development and progress of the continuing professional education provided by VERA. In this capacity he is also involved in the organisation of pan-European congresses such as Form 20F and MD&A, and US GAAP.

Since 1990 Verhoog has been the editor-in-chief of *VERA-Actueel*, the monthly continuing professional education magazine. He is editor-in-chief of 30 NIVRA/VERA books, of the annual VERA series *Actualiteiten in Accountancy* and the VERA series 'Fifteen expert opinions on …'. In 2000, *Strategic Finance in the 21st Century* was published as part of this series and has now been released on the international market under the title *A Vision for the Future* by the British publishing house John Wiley & Sons. A Chinese version was published in 2002 and a Russian edition of the book is also in production. Furthermore, Wiley, together with NIVRA/VERA will be publishing *Is Fair Value Fair?* (financial reporting from an international perspective), which will appear on the market at the same time as this book *Recent Trends in Valuation*.

Willem Verhoog has various other publications to his name.

Chapter 1

Introduction – strategic valuation:

The relationship between strategy, valuation techniques and options

Luc Keuleneer

Luc Keuleneer is a director at KPMG in Brussels, where he is responsible for strategic financial services. He is a member of the Supervisory Board of Valkieser Communications BU in Hilversum (The Netherlands). In addition, he is a judge in the Brussels Court of Commerce. He lectures at the Free University of Amsterdam, and the University of the Netherlands Antilles, Ghent University, Vlerick Leuven Gent Management School and the Catholic University of Leuven.

Willem Verhoog

Willem Verhoog has been the Secretary-general of Royal NIVRA'S VERA Committee since 1 August 1976. He is responsible for the development and progress of the continuing professional education of registeraccountants, provided by VERA.

One of the most important tasks in the management of a company is to provide direction to its future development. After a plan has been drawn up, its course should be followed. In other words, planning is followed by implementation and the desired development must be converted into practice. A vital precondition is a vision of the future concerning the company and its developments. A good manager is distinguished from less talented colleagues by his or her creativity and clarity of vision. These characteristics must result in a strategy that gives the company a lead over its competitors. The strategy must of course be a feasible one and capable of bringing the management's set goals within range. The latter is the essence of the process: undertaking action at all levels within the organisation, aimed at the realisation of the set objectives with the ultimate goal of creating value. It goes without saying that this will not be a static, annual exercise but an ongoing, dynamic process.

The strategy selected will therefore have a direct bearing on the financial performance of a company and hence on the creation of value for shareholders. This implies that the strategy must be developed to maximise the ability of the company to generate cash flows. Once this strategy has been formulated, shareholder value is created (or destroyed). That explains why an announced change in company strategy often has an effect on the share price, whereas nothing need as yet have changed in the actual activities and conduct of the business.

If the company is to be in a position to optimally focus its objectives and activities on the creation of value, a system will be required that makes it possible to direct, measure and evaluate in terms of value. It is now claimed that this system has been found in value-based management.

1. RELATIONSHIP BETWEEN VALUE-BASED MANAGEMENT AND VALUATION TECHNIQUES

1.1. From strategy ...

Value-based management (VBM) is a strategic/financial decision-making and management model that aims to maximise company value in the medium to long term. VBM makes it possible to define necessary strategic choices to increase the value of the company in the long term and seeks to assure the continuity of the company in the long term by creating and maximising shareholder value.

The success of a company is achieved in the commercial market. The company must deliver products and services sought by the market at a good price/quality ratio. In order to approach the commercial market, capital is required which is provided by the capital market in the form of equity and borrowed capital. For incurring a risk and deferring consumption, the providers of capital seek compensation in the form of capital gains, dividends or interest. The company must therefore be capable of generating sufficient financial resources in the commercial market (the operating cash flow) in order to meet the requirements of the capital providers (free cash flow).

A company is only successful and only creates shareholder value if it generates more financial resources than the capital providers expect (see Section 3.1 for a full explanation) or, in other words, if the operating result is higher in the long term than the return that the providers of equity and borrowed capital expect on their investment. In doing so account is of course taken of the risk-profile of the company's activities.

Two related core applications may be distinguished within the strategic/financial management model. These are:

- Shareholder value analysis (SVA) for the decision-making models; and
- Economic value added (EVA®) as a performance indicator for the management.

For the effective management of the organisation, it is vitally important that the decision-making and performance indicators are in line with one another. The internal management system of a company should therefore be directed towards the realisation of economic value and not towards the traditional concept of profit. The introduction of VBM makes it 'painfully' clear to managers and administrators that money is not free. It forces them radically to review their strategy and to assess whether each investment can produce a return.

But VBM can only generate good results if the management and the various business units display involvement in its implementation and if there is sufficient and reliable information on markets and the company's financial status. It is therefore highly important to ensure that value drivers provide the necessary insight and have practical utility for management.

1.2. ... to value

The shareholders in the company are the providers of risk capital. They want a return on the funds they have invested in the form of dividend distributions or increases in the value of the shares. In this way, the shareholder value corresponds with the shareholder return, which consists of two components: the dividend and the increase in value of the share. A company that wants to create value for shareholders must display a balance of future cash flows that is at least sufficient to fund the return sought. Two components need therefore to be estimated for calculating the value of the company: the future free cash flows (FCF) and the return required by the capital providers or weighted average cost of capital (WACC). It is the FCF that determine the value of the company. These cash flows must be available for the capital providers, especially for the shareholders and other capital providers. The value of a company is determined by calculating the present value of these free cash flows. By deducting the outstanding financial debts from the corporate value, one obtains the shareholder value. Calculating the value of a company in this way is called the discounted cash flow (DCF) method.

The scale of the value creation in a particular strategy is determined by the 'value drivers'. These latter determine the ability of the company to generate cash balances. Value drivers make it possible to calculate the current shareholder value, as well as the shareholder value of the optimal strategy. Seven factors are accepted in the literature as financial value drivers:

- Turnover growth.
- Operating margin.
- Investments in fixed assets.
- Investments in working capital.
- Duration of the competitive advantage.
- The cost of capital.
- The effective tax rate.

The WACC is particularly important. This is the weighted average of the cost of equity and borrowed capital. The cost of the equity capital consists of the risk-free return plus the systematic risk of the company (the beta) times the market risk premium. The cost of debt is the after-tax marginal cost to pay to the debt holder. The 'weighting ratio' employed is based on the proportions of equity and borrowed capital that the company has set itself as a goal (on the basis of the market value). Therefore, the capital structure (debt ratio, equity ratio) is an important element of the WACC. Since the two propositions of Modigliani and Miller, discussing the importance of the financial structure for the value of the company, efforts have been made in corporate finance to find the answer to the optimal capital structure of a company. An important conclusion is that due to the existence of market imperfections, such as taxes and bankruptcy costs, the optimal capital structure is bound up with the degree of debt financing. A company will, for example, be more inclined to borrow money if it is able to obtain interest relief. The ideal capital structure is therefore that which minimises the WACC, while taking account of the company's risk-profile.

2. OPTION THEORY IN THE DETERMINATION OF VALUE

A fine specific example of the interaction between financial policy in general and value determination in particular and fundamental scientific research is the increasing extent to which option theory is being applied.

The use of options theory in determining the value of companies may be summarised as follows: if today a call option is bought on a share X with an exercise price E, the value of that core option on the due date may be shown simply (see Figure 1.1).

The question that arises is: What has to be paid today in order to purchase such a call option? This may be calculated by using an option valuation model.

The same question can be posed in relation to a parcel of shares. What is their value today? Ultimately a share is nothing more than the right to the value of the company, after repayment of the borrowed capital.

The graph (Figure 1.2) showing the value of a call option on the due date of the call and that showing the value of the share on the due date of the borrowed capital are identical, except that the horizontal axis represents the value of the total company. For this reason the value of the share parcel *at this point* can be approximated in the same way as the calculation of the aforementioned call premium, in other words by an adjusted option valuation formula, in which use is of course made of corporate parameters. In addition, the model to be used will depend on the interest-bearing nature or otherwise of the borrowed capital. Shares are therefore in fact options.

Option theory is also making advances in investment analysis. In traditional investment analysis based on the net present value (NPV), account is often not taken of the real or strategic options. The latter can be the option to wait before investing and the option to make follow-up investments if the project succeeds, or what are known as growth options.

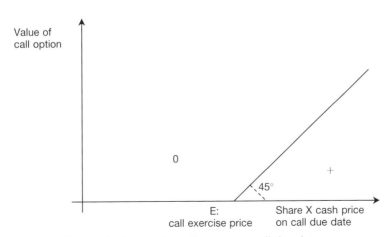

Figure 1.1 Value of a call option on call due date.

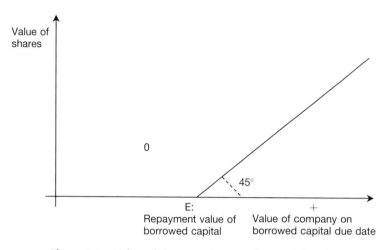

Figure 1.2   Value of shares on borrowed capital due date.

Many managers think that these options are not tangible and can only be taken into account qualitatively. This is not correct. These options are distinctly tangible and by implementation of the option theory in investment analysis a much better estimate can be made as to whether investments in R&D, the development of new markets and strategic takeovers – which in themselves do not look profitable – might nevertheless be worthwhile if the relationship is established with additional options and hence potential value they can generate. A company can therefore be considered as a portfolio of options – and shares of a company therefore as 'options on options'. This will be explained in depth in Chapters 2 and 3.

3. CONCLUSION

This book sets out to analyse various valuation techniques and recent refinements in a clear and comprehensible way and to examine the use of options theory in the determination of value (see Chapter 2 by Wouter De Maeseneire and Luc Keuleneer). All this is linked to its application in practice (see Chapter 3 by Tom Copeland). Finally, all this has been set in a strategic and integrated framework (see Chapter 4 by Geert Scheipers, Anne Ameels and Werner Bruggeman).

Valuation of companies

Discounted cash flow, adjusted present value, decision-tree analysis and real options

Wouter De Maeseneire

Wouter De Maeseneire has a degree in Applied Economics at Ghent University, Belgium. He has been a research assistant at the Competence Centre Accounting & Finance of the Vlerick Leuven Gent Management School. He is currently an Aspirant of the Fund for Scientific Research-Flanders (FWO-Vlaanderen) and is a PhD candidate at the Department of Corporate Finance, Faculty of Economics and Business Administration, Ghent University. He is also a visiting researcher at Erasmus University Rotterdam, the Netherlands. His research focuses on valuation issues, real options, initial public offerings and private equity.

Luc Keuleneer

Luc Keuleneer is a director at KPMG in Brussels, where he is responsible for strategic financial services. He is a member of the Supervisory Board of Valkieser Communications BU in Hilversum (The Netherlands). In addition, he is a judge in the Brussels Court of Commerce. He lectures at the Free University of Amsterdam, and the University of the Netherlands Antilles, Ghent University, Vlerick Leuven Gent Management School and the Catholic University of Leuven.

1. INTRODUCTION

It is important to know the correct value of a company and its shares within the context of mergers and acquisitions, raising new equity and initial public offerings. This information is also relevant in the case of disputes between different parties (for example, conflicts with minority shareholders in public buyout offers, where discussions take place on a regular basis about whether they get a fair price for their shares). The value of a company must also sometimes be determined for tax purposes.

The valuation of companies is essential for many business decisions and should be properly applied. Therefore, the most important valuation methods will be defined and illustrated in this chapter. Indications will also be given of when to use which method and of the shortcomings of each method. It is not the intention to provide a complete overview of all existing valuation methods. Adjusted net asset value, the dividend discount model, the use of multiples or market ratios and other methods are deliberately excluded. Adjusted net asset value does not determine the going concern value but rather the liquidation value. The dividend discount model is mathematically equal to the discounted cash flow (DCF), but harder to use in practice (for example, inconsistencies between dividends and future growth, which are interrelated). Multiples do not rely on a fundamental basis and assume that the company can be compared to the peer group to a large extent, and that this peer group is valued correctly. These assumptions are often doubtful and subject to a lot of debate.

The aim of this chapter is, then, to comment on, to illustrate and provide a critique on the more advanced valuation models, which are generally accepted or are all the rage in the literature, the academic world and in practice, and make clear the main differences between the techniques. In addition, indications will be given of the context in which each valuation method can be used in order to estimate the value of an enterprise in a well-founded manner.

The first model discussed is DCF. Before other valuation methods can be considered, one has to master this widely accepted basic model. Those other methods are based on the strengths of DCF, but in addition explicitly make allowance for its shortcomings. The DCF model and its constituting elements are examined. In particular, attention will be paid to the determination of the cost of equity. The second model, and one that provides an initial critique on the DCF method, is the adjusted present value method (APV). Decision-tree analysis (DTA) and the real options method (RO) will subsequently be discussed. These provide a further critique of the DCF model that cannot be remedied with the APV model. After this, the weaknesses associated with valuation on the basis of the real options method will be discussed. The chapter ends with a summary and conclusions. Based on this chapter the reader has an update of all recent trends in valuation. The discussion in Chapter 3 is about the application in practice of the techniques.

2. DISCOUNTED CASH FLOW METHOD

2.1. Description of the DCF method

A valuation technique that is dealt with in all corporate finance manuals, the DCF method is taught at all universities and business schools. In practice, it seems to be the most popular method for the valuation of both individual projects and entire companies: the value of an enterprise is equal to the discounted value of all future free operating cash flows generated by that enterprise. A brief outline is given of the essence of the DCF method and a number of important comments will be made about its key parameters.

The free operating cash flow is the operating cash flow less the necessary investments in both fixed assets and net operating capital requirements. This shows what the company can distribute each year to shareholders and creditors, without endangering its continuity. The following schedule shows how free operating cash flow is computed.[1]

> EBIT (Earnings before interest and taxes)
>   − Operating taxes (Calculated as: EBIT × tax rate (t))
>   = NOPLAT (Net operating profit less adjusted taxes)
>   + Depreciation and amortisation
>   = Operating cash flow
>   − Investments in fixed assets[2]
>   − Investments in net operating capital requirements
>   = Free operating cash flow

The free operating cash flows are discounted at the opportunity cost of capital invested in the company: that is, the weighted average cost of capital (WACC), which can be computed as follows:

$$\text{WACC} = C_E \times E/V + C_D \times (1 - t) \times D/V$$

As can be seen, the weighted cost of equity (C_E) and debt (C_D) (cost of debt after taxes (t = tax rate), because the interest charges are tax

---

[1] This should be indirectly determined because the figure cannot be directly deduced from financial statements.

[2] Or disinvestments; if the company sells one of its assets in a given year, the result would be an additional positive cash flow, and thus a higher free operating cash flow. Of course, the question is whether the asset sale will negatively affect results and cash flows in subsequent years. In the projections of these elements, this question should explicitly be taken into account.

deductible) is calculated in accordance with the relative target proportions[3] (E/V and D/V where V = total market value of capital, E = equity
and D = interest bearing debt), measured at market value, in the company's capital structure. The above formula can easily be adjusted for more
complex capital structures (for example, preferred stock).

After discounting (and summing) all future free operating cash flows,
one arrives at the (operational) value for the entire company. The value of
non-operating assets, such as marketable securities, must be added to
this. Cash inflows of those assets must not be included in the above
schedule of operating cash flows (which is normally not the case),
because they would otherwise be counted twice. To find the value of
shares, that is, the value of equity, the market value of debt is subtracted
from the total firm value referred to above.

2.2. Projected free operating cash flows

Of course, it is impossible to estimate the future free operating cash flow
for each year separately. Therefore, a projection period will be introduced.
An explicit expression of the expected cash flow will be stated, based on
the company's business plan, projected balance sheets, profit and loss
accounts and liquidity positions. The necessary inputs can be derived
from these sources in order to substantiate the above-mentioned free
operating cash flows computation scheme. The projection period is generally a period of 5 to 10 years, preferably as long as possible, so that a
well-founded projection can be made. After this projection period, a final
value, or continuing value, is filled in. The point of departure here is that
either the company will generate the estimated free operating cash flow
during the final year of the explicit projection period to infinity or that this
cash flow will keep on increasing at a constant growth rate (thus leading
to a perpetuity; this value must also be discounted). If necessary, alternatives can be formulated with different growth rates for different periods
in the future, but this rarely occurs.

When determining the continuing value, care should be taken that the
company at that moment has more or less reached maturity, because the
main assumption is that it has a constant growth rate from that moment

---

[3] One has to use a 'target', a desired capital structure that the company will
maintain on average in the future, even if the actual structure differs from this
target. The valuation is made in accordance with the projections for all periods in
the future and it is therefore better to use the average capital structure that the
company will maintain in the future, and to base the calculations of the WACC on
this. An actual short-lived deviation of the desired structure must not influence the
valuation (see also the APV method).

on (maybe even a zero growth rate), which is maintained until infinity. For many companies, this final value determines a major part of their total value.[4] It is therefore very important that the elements of the continuing value are estimated precisely, and this is not always obvious. The free operating cash flow can be derived from the forecasts for the projection period. The weighted average cost of capital has already been discussed (and will be dealt with in more detail in Chapter 3). It is essential to estimate the growth of a company as accurately as possible in the long run; it is, for instance, totally unrealistic to take a long-term growth rate of 12%; no company can maintain such growth to infinity. One must keep in mind that this growth rate must be in the region of the average growth rate of the economy; all companies together grow on average in line with the economy as a whole – some slower, some faster – but the deviations must not be too large, otherwise (taken to infinity), a company would become larger than the entire economy. Usually, nominal growth rates are used as most elements within the DCF model are expressed in nominal terms (sales, personnel costs, risk free rate, . . .); alternatively, real growth rates can be used if all other figures are in real terms too.

As with all models, 'garbage in, garbage out' also holds for this theoretically well-founded method. If the business plan and the free operating cash flow based upon it are unrealistic, then the derived computed 'value' will also be unrealistic. The same applies to the growth rate; suppose the WACC is 6% and a growth rate of 4% is taken instead of 2%, what may seem a small deviation at first sight produces a continuing value that is twice as high. The correctness of these parameters is the main point and one must be careful of overvaluations.

2.3. Essential for the WACC: the cost of equity

This section will not cover all constituent components of the WACC, but focus on the cost of equity, since this is the most difficult element to estimate and errors can very easily be made. The capital asset pricing model (CAPM), the small firm premium (SFP) and the arbitrage pricing theory (APT) will be discussed in order to determine this particular parameter.

---

[4] For traditional companies with limited growth, a substantial part of the value is captured in the explicit projection period; for a lot of rapidly growing technology companies, the value of the cash flows in the projection period is negative, and more than 100% of today's total value is contained in the continuing value.

Capital Asset Pricing Model (CAPM)

Using the CAPM, the cost of equity, the minimum required return for shareholders, can be calculated by means of the following formula:

$$C_E = r_f + \text{equity beta} \times [r_m - r_f]$$

[handwritten annotation above formula: 6.5% − 1.5~2% survivorship bias]

This can be expressed as follows: the shareholders require a return that is at least equal to the risk-free interest rate (r_f), increased by a premium for the risk they take. Here (equity) beta indicates the amount of risk of the company's shares and ($r_m - r_f$) is the price of risk, the risk premium. In general, risk is measured by fluctuations in the value of a share, and more precisely, by the variance (or standard deviation) of the returns. The amount of risk of a share in a well-diversified portfolio (beta) is determined by the sensitivity of the return of a share, relative to market movements. A share that fluctuates more than the market has a beta higher than 1 (aggressive shares, for example, those held in the semiconductor industry) and a potential investor will require a higher return for this. A beta less than 1 (including the more traditional and stable sectors, such as energy) indicates that a share fluctuates less than the market, therefore contains less risk and requires a lower return than an investment in the market portfolio.

Why is allowance only made of the risk of fluctuations, as a function of how the market moves (the so-called systematic, non-diversifiable risk, measured by the beta), and not of the total risk? Total risk takes every fluctuation into consideration, thus both the systematic and non-systematic[5] risk related to an enterprise and its shares. The answer is simple if one takes a look at Figure 2.1: the total risk of a portfolio is a function of the number of shares in the portfolio. It is immediately apparent that the risk of a portfolio decreases rapidly as the number of shares in the portfolio rises; the reason for this is that the fluctuations of shares are not perfectly correlated with each other. If a particular share increases in price, another will decrease in value or increase to a lesser extent. The fluctuations of individual shares partly compensate one another, so the risk of a portfolio is much lower than the risk of an individual share. This is the theory of Markowitz (1959): by diversifying the portfolio, by including a large number of shares, the risk will be reduced. If a portfolio is sufficiently diversified, its risk will equal the market risk. Since the total risk can be reduced to market risk – the systematic risk that cannot be diversified – in perfect capital markets if the shares are well spread, the capital market only offers compensation for the systematic

---

[5] This risk is also referred to as the idiosyncratic or diversifiable risk.

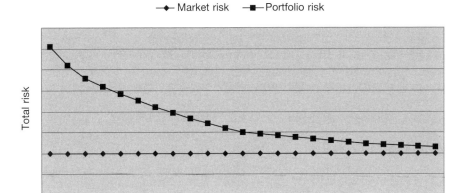

Figure 2.1 Total risk of a portfolio of shares.

risk incurred. Therefore, the level of risk is not measured by the total fluctuations of a share (total volatility), but by the level of fluctuation relative to the market portfolio, which contains all possible risky assets. In other words, consideration is taken of the level of volatility expressed in relation to the volatility of the market.

The beta for listed shares can be determined by performing a regression analysis of the returns of a specific share on the market returns (usually a representative stock market price index). This way of working assumes that the past is representative for the future. If the company or the sector has undergone fundamental changes that affect the market risk, account can best be taken of this by adjusting the beta as a function of this modified risk profile. For unlisted shares (for example, in the case of an initial public offering), a beta will be estimated on the basis of comparable, listed companies. Here as well, an adjustment can be helpful to correct for differences between the company to be valued and the reference group used.

It is also essential that a distinction be made between the equity beta (also referred to as levered beta) and the asset beta (unlevered beta) of an enterprise. The relationship between asset and equity beta is given by:

$$\text{Equity beta} = \text{Asset beta} \times [1 + (1 - t)D/E]$$

where D/E is the ratio of debt to equity (measured in market values) and t is the tax rate. This formula says that the equity beta increases as a function of the level of the company's debt financing (there is a fiscal advantage associated with this, see the factor $(1 - t))$ and as a function of the asset beta. The asset beta only takes account of the degree of risk[6] of the operations, the risk profile of the assets on the left-hand side of the balance sheet. In addition to this operating risk, however, a company also faces financial risk, according to the level of debt financing, which is reflected in the right-hand side of the balance sheet. The equity beta incorporates both risks in a single measure; it is this equity beta that should be used as an input for the CAPM. When looking at comparable companies to estimate beta, the average financial risk of the reference group and the financial risk of the company to be valued should be taken into consideration. This is referred to as unlevering, to determine asset beta, and relevering, to take the capital structure of the firm that needs to be valued into consideration.

The risk premium (or equity premium), $r_m - r_f$, is the expected return of the market portfolio on top of the risk-free investment. Historically, measured over a long period, this risk premium amounts to 6.5% (see Copeland *et al.*, 2000). This is, however, the actually realised return and represents an overestimate of the expected return, since only the survivors remain in the indices used to compute the market return and unsuccessful companies are frequently removed. This leads to an ex-post realised return that is higher than the expected ex-ante return. After adjustment of the measured risk premium for this 'survivorship bias', which is estimated at 1.5% to 2%, a risk premium of 4% to 5% is obtained. Fama and French (2002) use dividend and earnings growth rates to measure equity premiums and find a risk premium ranging from 2.55% to 4.32% for the period 1951–2000. According to the specific methodology and time period used, different outcomes are obtained.

It should be pointed out that the above remark also applies to beta, for which different values are obtained on each occasion, depending upon the basic past period used to estimate these parameters and the specific estimation method. An accurate valuation will only be produced if these parameters are representative of the parameters currently requested by the market (and in the future). In many cases, however, historical estimates do provide a close approximation, but this comment should always be kept in mind.

In practice, the CAPM is the most frequently used method for determining the cost of equity. Nevertheless, not everybody is convinced of the effectiveness of this model. In various studies it has been shown that not only the systematic risk explains the actual return, but that other elements have explanatory power as well. These will be discussed in the next two sections.

---

[6] This degree of risk is expressed relative to the market.

Small Firm Premium (SFP)

As early as 1981, Blanz (1981) and Reinganum (1981) had observed that besides beta, the size[7] of the company was also important to explain a cross-section of actual returns. The smaller the firm, the higher the actual return, even for different betas. A famous article by Fama and French in 1992 even went so far as to state that beta was of no value to explain the returns. These authors believe that the size (negative relationship) of an enterprise and the ratio of the book value to the market value (positive relationship) explain the returns, and not beta. Reinganum (1992) found that in the long run small companies have an average return that is 13% higher than that of large companies.

There are a number of reasons why small companies are riskier than large companies, and why a Small Firm Premium (SFP) needs to be introduced (Van der Heijden, 1999). A Small Firm has a greater chance of failure, there is less information available, which leads to greater un-certainty and higher information gathering costs (these shares are less important to analysts) and the shares are less liquid. The bid-ask spreads and thus the transaction costs for smaller shares are higher. Silber (1991) finds a discount of no less than 33.75% for so-called re-stricted shares (which temporarily must not be traded) in relation to non-restricted shares. Another clear example of the role of liquidity is given by Amihud, Mendelson and Lauterbach (1997): the shares on the Israeli stock market, which were converted from one-day trading to con-tinuous trading, gained on average 5.5% as a result of an increase in liquidity (and a decrease in required return). Brennan and Tamarowski (2000) found a difference in required return between the most and the least liquid shares (measured through the bid-ask spread) of 6.89% on an annual basis; they consider the size of a company to be the strongest factor in determining the number of analysts following it. The shares that attract the largest number of analysts have the lowest trading costs and the highest traded volumes, and thus the highest liquidity. Therefore, evidence suggests that a large company has a lower required return.

However, there has been considerable debate about the SFP. It has been argued that the higher risk premium for smaller firms is found because of measurement errors and survivorship bias in the model used, and because of correlation between the small firm effect and other stock market anomalies. Kothari, Shanken and Sloan (1995), for example, state that if the above-mentioned effects are corrected for,

---

[7] In various studies, factors other than beta have been found that help to explain the returns: the January effect, the day-of-the-week effect, etc. These are less relevant here, however.

beta is very significant to explain the returns. The size effect is significant but the impact is only minimal. The book value/market value ratio does not influence the actual returns. Many arguments can therefore be given for including the SFP in the required return, but there are arguments against it as well. Based on a study of the available empirical data and economic theory (which both tend to shift the balance towards a higher required return for small firms), KPMG in the Netherlands uses an average additional premium of 2.5% for listed companies and 4.0% for private companies.

Arbitrage Pricing Theory (APT)

APT is a multifactor model. It is analogous to the CAPM, which is a one-factor model explaining returns on the basis of one systematic risk factor (Copeland *et al.*, 2000) – that is, the market return and the sensitivity of a company's shares with respect to this factor (beta). On the other hand, APT models make use of several underlying economic factors that determine the systematic risk and the sensitivity of a share to each of these fundamental risk factors, in order to explain the returns (several beta coefficients). Empirically, changes in the following risk factors prove to be very important (Chen, Roll and Ross, 1986): index of industrial production, short-term real interest rate, short-term inflation, long-term inflation and default risk. Financial institutions seem, for example, to be very sensitive (high beta coefficient for this independent variable) to (unexpected) changes in long-term inflation. Another variant of APT determines, via factor analysis, which uncorrelated factors are important to explain returns. A main disadvantage of this statistical way of working is that the resulting factors are very difficult or impossible to interpret. The question arises: What economic variable lies behind these factors?

It is seen that APT models are better able than the CAPM to explain returns. The other side of the coin, however, is that APT models are more complex and that important factors or sensitivities with respect to these factors (beta coefficients) for many companies are not known. And APT models can certainly be used as an alternative for the CAPM, but their application is not always evident. Therefore, APT models are rarely used in practice to determine the cost of equity.

2.4. Importance of WACC in EVA[®][8]

Bearing in mind the comments in the sections above, and based on the correct application of the CAPM (or perhaps an APT model), the cost of

---

[8] EVA[®] is a registered trademark of Stern Stewart & Co.

equity is determined; this cost may contain a small firm premium. The cost of equity, together with the other parameters, lead via the WACC formula to the weighted average cost of capital invested in the firm. A comparison of the cost of capital invested in a firm with the return that a company realises on this capital is the essence of an economic value added (EVA®) analysis. The EVA® of a firm during a particular period is measured by:

$$\text{EVA}^{®} = (\text{ROIC} - \text{WACC}) \times \text{Invested capital}$$

The WACC is the cost of capital, ROIC stands for 'return on invested capital' (NOPLAT/Invested capital) and invested capital equals fixed assets and net working capital; that is, the balance sheet total. Economic value is created if the invested resources yield more than they cost. The WACC is an essential input for an EVA®[9] analysis. Also, EVA® analysis can be used for valuation purposes: the sum of all future EVA®s a company will generate determines its current market value. Mathematically, this method is equivalent to DCF.

2.5. Enterprise DCF versus equity DCF

The method referred to here as enterprise (entity) DCF starts with a company's total free cash flows (the cash flows accruing to both the shareholders' equity and debt holders), and discounts these at the WACC, to compute the value of the company as a whole. The value of equity is the company's value minus the value of debt. This is the most frequently used of the DCF models, and is appropriate for most companies and applications. There is a second possibility, however: the equity DCF model. The free operating cash flows that accrue to the shareholders are discounted immediately at the required return of stockholders, that is, the cost of equity. The value of equity is thus obtained directly. These cash flows accruing to the shareholders are to a large extent the same as in the enterprise DCF model, but are after deduction of the repayments of loans and interest charges (cash flows to the debt holders). The two models are mathematically identical. In most cases the enterprise DCF method is preferable, however. A company derives its value in first instance from the operations it performs[10] and not as much from its financing activities, because almost all companies raise financing at market conditions. Furthermore, by applying enterprise DCF, improved

$V_E = V - V_D$

the most *Enterprise DCF*

---

[9] 'Economic profit' is identical to EVA®.
[10] This distinction between the creation of value by operations on the one hand and financing activities on the other is very clear in the APV method.

insight is gained into exactly where and how value is created, and it is more appropriate if numerous business units are valued (according to the equity DCF model, debt and interest charges must be explicitly assigned to business units and this is not always obvious). In addition, with equity DCF the mistake is easily made of not adjusting the cost of equity to a higher dividend payment, which implies a higher level of debt, and the (wrong) conclusion is frequently drawn that paying out more to shareholders increases the value of a company's shares.

However, the equity DCF method is preferable for financial institutions, such as banks, because their own financing activities and the active and thorough management of their liabilities are part of their essential operations, and the associated cash flows can thus better be included in the numerator of our model (instead of being incorporated in the valuation model via the WACC, the denominator). A principal source of financing for these institutions is the use of client deposits, which are accompanied by little or no interest charges. The interest charges vary between institutions. A bank therefore does not finance itself entirely at market conditions. Banks differ significantly in how well they utilise this source of funds, so that differences in value creation occur, thus not only on the assets side (as in the case of a normal company), but also on the liabilities side. Both of these are very important for a financial institution. Furthermore, the costs of specific forms of financing for financial institutions are difficult to estimate, and the spreads between a bank's interest payments and its own financing costs are so small that a small percentage error in the estimation of these costs would lead to an enormous difference in value. It is therefore better to make these costs and cash flows more explicit.

2.6. Where can specific valuation parameters be found?

Many of the parameters required to make a valuation can be found in the business plan of a company and in past, current and projected financial statements. A thorough analysis of the past is often made in order to better estimate the future. 'Insider information' is often needed to make an accurate valuation; publicly available information will not suffice. Many parameters (for example, estimated betas, company market capitalisations, risk premium, risk free interest, peer groups), which may serve as a starting point, can be obtained from financial websites (for example, Bloomberg, Reuters, Stockpoint), stock exchange websites, reports of analysts and studies of financial institutions, suppliers of information and databases (such as Datastream), financial newspapers and investment magazines.

2.7. Critique of the DCF method

The DCF method does have some disadvantages and can be criticised from two different points of view. The APV (adjusted present value) method offers a solution for the first potential disadvantage; DTA (decision-tree analysis) and RO (real options) provide an answer for a second and fundamentally more severe drawback of the standard DCF method.

3. ADJUSTED PRESENT VALUE METHOD

3.1. Description of the APV method

The valuation of the APV method states that the value of a company is equal to the 'base' value of the operations plus the value of all the financial side-effects (Luehrman, 1997a, b).

> Value of company = Base value of operations
> + Value of financial side-effects

The 'base' value of the operating activities is determined by means of the value of the free operating cash flows (identical to those used in enterprise DCF), discounted at the cost of equity, as if the company was financed entirely with equity. This is therefore the (unlevered) cost of equity based on the asset beta, which only reflects the risk of the operations. By financing entirely with equity, asset and equity beta are equal to one another. Subsequently, an explicit estimate is made of the value of all financial side-effects, such as the tax shields on interest charges, possible grants, financial guarantees, as well as potential bankruptcy costs, specific risk management policies and issue costs. The value of these financial side-effects is obtained by estimating the associated cash flows and discounting these at a rate reflecting the risks related to each of these cash flows. The value of tax-deductible interest charges, for example, is usually determined on the basis of a discount rate equal to the cost of debt (before taxes), assuming that the corresponding cash flows, the projected annual tax benefits, are almost as risky as the debt repayments and interest charges associated with the debt. If the corresponding cash flows have a high degree of risk, a higher discount rate must be used. In the literature, there is a lot of debate about the correct discount rate for the financial side-effects. The central point is that the APV method makes the value of these financial side-effects more explicit by presenting them separately in cash flow projections, discounting them correctly, and adding them to the value of the operations. The DCF method incorporates the value of the financial effects by discounting the value of the operations (the free operating cash flows) at a lower WACC that is adjusted for financial side-effects. In this step, the adjustment of the WACC, things may go wrong.

The main added value of the APV method is that it provides clear insight into how the total value of a company is calculated (operations versus financing), which is not the case with the DCF method. An additional problem with the enterprise DCF approach is that it is not so obvious how the WACC can be correctly estimated or how it can be properly adjusted for all financial side-effects, except in the case of simple financing structures. This can better be circumvented by explicitly estimating these financial cash flows year by year, as is done in the APV method. An example can clarify this. In the WACC formula, the cost of debt is immediately adjusted for tax deductibility $[C_D \times (1 - t)]$. However, what if this tax advantage is only effectively realised after a few years, because the company, for instance, incurs losses during the first few years? A second example also quickly comes to mind: the WACC and thus the tax advantage of financing debt is computed in accordance with the long-term target capital structure. No allowance is made for actual deviations because only one WACC is used. This can easily be solved with the APV method by determining the cash flows for each year considering the changes in the actual capital structure, and by only including the realised tax advantages. Dynamic capital structures therefore often lead to errors in a DCF valuation as an incorrect WACC is used. Leveraged buyouts provide a good example of a non-constant capital structure where APV is preferred.

The WACC approach is thus too simplified in most cases and is based on assumptions which are not always true: all financial side-effects are incorporated in one adjusted discount rate, which has the advantage of being straightforward, but which easily causes errors. With complex financing structures, and when using less acceptable forms of debt financing, such as convertible bonds and loans with variable interest rates, the probability of estimating a wrong value for the financial securities with the WACC is rather high. This in any case applies to companies that are confronted with a complicated tax situation.

Another important advantage of the APV method is that the value of the operations can be split up and that the value of potential operational changes (for example, reduction of the net working capital requirement, marginal improvement by means of a more efficient IT system) can be unequivocally estimated, because each of these corresponding cash flows is discounted at the same cost of equity (as if the company were 100% equity financed). With the WACC approach, a different WACC for each of the proposed changes has to be determined, depending upon the associated degree of risk. The advantage of APV compared to DCF via the WACC is also straightforward in the valuation of, for example, a foreign acquisition. The value of such an acquisition is the value of the operational activities, plus the value of any grants that will be received, subsidised local forms of financing, special financial advantages and tax concessions.

Finally, it should be noted that the outcome of the enterprise DCF method, which uses the WACC, is mathematically identical to that of the APV method when it is correctly applied and all assumptions are identical.

3.2. Critique of the APV method

The APV method offers a number of important advantages. It provides a clear insight into the sources of value creation and the errors inherent to the WACC approach are avoided by not incorporating the value of financial side-effects in the WACC, but by making them explicit. However, a crucial aspect of the APV method remains the accurate determination of the value of the financial side-effects. The potential bankruptcy costs associated with the degree of debt financing are often overlooked or wrongly estimated. Of course, this has a major impact on valuation. Other side-effects affecting valuation are not always included correctly in the analysis as well.

3.3. Critique of DCF and APV

Both DCF and APV can be used to value 'assets-in-place', or current assets, but they are not methods capable of taking account of the value of 'opportunities', or the real options at a company's disposal. This is dealt with in more detail in the remainder of this chapter.

4. DECISION-TREE ANALYSIS (DTA) AND REAL OPTIONS (RO)

4.1. Observations

The market value of many companies is much higher than the value computed in accordance with a DCF (or APV) analysis (see, for example, Smit and Trigeorgis, 1992). This is due to the fact that the DCF method only evaluates and values existing activities, while the market also considers the options, the 'opportunities', which a company has and which lead to additional value. Especially in technological and innovative sectors (such as IT, electronics and pharmaceuticals), with a higher level of uncertainty, a great deal of the value is determined by the portfolio of future options that these companies have at their disposal, and not as much by their current activities. The value of Internet companies, biotechnology companies and many start-ups is also based on future potential activities (options) that they may be able to perform and not as much on their current (usually loss-making) activities.

4.2. Wrong interpretations of the DCF method (and APV method)

(1) The DCF method uses expected cash flows that are estimated at a particular point in time, given the current general economic, industry and firm specific circumstances that companies rely on to determine the way they will operate. The DCF model is, however, very rigid and assumes that the company and its management do not have any flexibility (and therefore underestimates the value of a good management team) and thus can no longer reconsider previous decisions if the circumstances appear to change and new information is available. This is incorrect in almost all situations: companies can certainly adapt to and take advantage of changed situations. Projects and decisions made in the past are not entirely irreversible. Suppose that a certain project does not turn out as expected and generates negative cash flows, a decision will then have to be taken whether to discontinue the project, if this is one of the possibilities (options). If this is the case, the previously determined negative or low cash flows are too pessimistic; the initial estimated expected cash flow thus actually systematically (if there are options) underestimates the cash flow that is subsequently actually generated, and so underestimates the value of projects and companies. Conversely, suppose that a project goes well and generates enormous positive cash flows. An attempt will then be made to expand the project (for example, by working over-time and by opening up new markets) so that the originally estimated positive cash flows will also turn out to be too low. If there are 'opportunities' and the company can take advantage of these, which is usually the case, then the expected cash flow used in the DCF model will be too low, resulting in an undervaluation.

(2) The DCF method is also inadequate for the evaluation of projects and activities that may not be profitable in themselves, but which in case of success permit the making of very profitable follow-up investments (an example of this is R&D for the discovery of new medicines). The follow-up (3) project should be seen as an option and therefore be valued as one. A final important difference is the role of uncertainty (volatility): with the DCF method, this leads to a higher required return and a lower value, whereas option valuation will result in a higher value for projects with a higher

degree of risk. This is caused by different assumptions: the DCF model assumes a symmetric distribution of the cash flow results; option valuation assumes an asymmetric distribution (only the positive results). This will be discussed in more detail below.

4.3. Real options and the analogy with financial options

By means of real options (RO) a value is therefore assigned to the options at the management's disposal. The total value of a company is formulated in the so-called 'extended DCF rule': the value according to a static DCF (or APV) analysis increased with the value of all these options (dynamic component). These option values can be determined in a manner that is similar to the valuation techniques for financial options. A summary of the models for option valuation is described by Amram and Kulatilaka (1999). There are three categories of solution methods: by solving the partial differential equation (for example, the Black and Scholes model), dynamic programming (for example, the binomial model of option valuation) and by means of simulations (for example, Monte Carlo simulations). The value of all the options that are at a company's disposal is, however, not equal to the sum of the values of the individual options because they interact.[11] As a general rule, binomial trees are more applicable in real option valuation than the Black and Scholes formula, as they allow the valuation of various options simultaneously and put less restrictions on the distribution of the underlying value.

In Table 2.1, the corresponding parameters,[12] which are important for real options and financial options, are compared to each other. Because of these parallels, real options can be valued in the same way as options on financial assets. An option on a share gives the right to buy (call option) or to sell (put option) an underlying share during a specific period (American option) or at the end of that period (European option) at a predetermined price. As this concerns a 'right', the value of an option can never be negative, because then the holder of the option does not exercise the right. This accounts for the positive influence of risk (volatility) in the valuation of options: the 'loss' is limited to a zero value; the potential profit is very high and increases as uncertainty increases. Therefore, an asymmetric pay-off arises. The value of a call option increases with $S - X$ and r_f, with an increase in the duration t, with a higher volatility σ, and decreases with dividends paid out

---

[11] A shrinking option and a stopping option, for example, partially overlap and are valuable in the same situations: their value, examined together, is therefore much lower than the sum of their individual values.

[12] These parameters are sufficient to calculate the value of an option.

Table 2.1 Investment opportunity/Real option.

Investment opportunity	Option on a share
Present value of the free cash flows generated by the project[13]	Price of the underlying share (S)
Investments required to carry out the project (or disinvestment amount)	Exercise price of the option (X)
For what period of time does the company have this opportunity?	Duration of the option (t)
Time value of money (given by the risk-free interest rate)	Risk-free interest rate (r_f)
Degree of risk of the project	Volatility of the underlying share (σ)
Lost cash flows due to not immediately committing to the project	Dividends paid (d)

Source: Copeland and Antikarov, 2001.

d.[14] This is applied and discussed for an option to expand an investment project (comparable with a call option). The expansion option is more valuable if the project will generate more cash flows (S) or if the required investments for the project are lower (X), in the case of an increase in the volatility (σ) of the cash flows of the project and in the case of a longer period during which the company can decide whether to expand or not (t). All of these real option parameters should be determined by explicitly taking the competitive setting into consideration. For instance, the value and duration of an expansion option will depend on whether or not (and to what extent) competitors are considering expansion. Allowance can be made for the role of competition by integrating game theoretic principles within real option valuation.

4.4. When is the value of real options important?

The value of real options is important in all situations where there is considerable uncertainty about the future, and where it is likely that new information will be available after a period of time, and where the management has sufficient flexibility to make allowance for this and take advantage of it. Obviously, this is often the case in real life business contexts. The value of real options is less important in situations where

---

[13] This is nothing more than a DCF value and forms an essential input for the valuation of options!

[14] The value of a put option increases with $X - S$, t, σ, d, and decreases with r_f.

Table 2.2 Summary of types of real options: the 7 S framework.

To invest/grow further (CALL)	Scale up	Expand project as the market grows
	Switch up	Expand project to the following generation of a product/technology
	Scope up	Extend investment to other applications and industries
To postpone/learn (CALL)	Study/start	Postpone investment until more information is released or capabilities are obtained
Disinvest/cut back (PUT)	Scale down	Stop or cut back project if new information is released that reduces the expected cash flows
	Switch down	Switch to more cost-efficient and more flexible assets in new circumstances
	Scope down	Reduce the scope of a project (perhaps completely) if the potential in that activity is insufficient

Source: Copeland and Keenan, 1998a.

the net present value is very positive or negative, because the decision that management will take will not change when the value of real options is allowed for (Copeland and Keenan, 1998b). For this kind of project, there is only a slight possibility that a previously taken decision or strategy will be reconsidered.

4.5. What types of real options exist?

To value a company from a real options perspective, each of its real options (Table 2.2) for all the company projects should be detected and valued. Of course, this is hardly feasible and one will focus on those real options that are really relevant and have a major impact. A few examples of real options are given below (see Section 4.7).

4.6. From decision-tree analysis (DTA) to real options

The transition from DCF to real options is made by means of decision-tree analysis (DTA). These concepts show, from a value maximising perspective, which investment (or disinvestment) decisions will be taken, given all possible future market circumstances. By making use of a decision tree, it is possible to map out how the initial basic investment decision and strategy will be adjusted at certain decision points as time passes, new events occur and new information is available. This diagram[15] provides a summary of all potential market circumstances (events), the probability that one of these scenarios will occur, the related cash flows and the corresponding investment decisions that will be taken. This first step facilitates the making of a DCF analysis based on these decision trees. The decision-tree based DCF value is already more accurate than the original DCF valuation. This is because the expected cash flows are more accurately estimated and allowance is made for the value of opportunities that a company can and will take advantage of. The problem, however, is that this method leads to an overestimation of value because, for each of these scenarios and further investment decisions, the discount rate is the same as that used for the original basic investment project. This therefore supposes an equal degree of risk, which is incorrect. The subsequent decisions are options, which are by nature subject to leverage,[16] and are therefore more risky than the underlying investment project itself. It is therefore both incorrect to use the discount rate of the original project and to suppose that it is constant over time. The correct discount rate is usually much higher than the one used to evaluate the basic investment.

4.7. A few examples of real options

In this section a number of valuation applications, making use of real option models, are presented.[17] The examples are consciously made relatively easy, and are based on a number of simplifying assumptions to make them as clear as possible. More realistic and more comprehensive examples make matters much more complex. It is particularly important to understand the intuition and underlying principles for differences in valuation between real options and DCF. The exact method for calculating real option values are not covered in detail here.

The option to wait

A frequent option is the option to wait before making an investment until new information is known. DCF always regards an investment as a

---

[15] An example of a decision tree is given in the valuation of an R&D project, following the real options method (see 'Valuation of an R&D project', p. 28).
[16] An option on a share always fluctuates more than the underlying asset itself.
[17] See also Copeland and Antikarov (2001), a very good manual about real options, containing many applications.

now-or-never decision, which is not very realistic, because management usually has the flexibility to make the investment later on when market circumstances have changed. A very simple but concise example shows the difference between the two methods.

Suppose that a company could invest in a perpetual project, requiring an initial expense of US$1,000 and a return of 10%. There are two possible situations, each with an equal chance of occurring (50%): either the market is favourable and the project generates free cash flows of US$150 each year, or it is unfavourable with annual cash flows of US$50. These market conditions will only be known one year from now. A DCF approach (present value of expected free cash flows – initial investment) produces the following value: $50\% \times$ (US$150/ $10\%) + 50\% \times$ (US$50/10%) – US$1,000 = US$0. But now suppose that management has the flexibility to wait one year before deciding whether to undertake the project or not. If the market is favourable, the value of the project within one year is: (US$150/10%) – US$1,000 = US$ 500. If the market is unfavourable, at first sight a value within one year is found of: (US$50/10%) – US$1,000 = –US$500. In these circumstances, however, the decision will be taken not to go through with the project and the value is therefore USD 0. After all, the company has the right, the option, to determine whether or not to undertake the project and will not do so if the value is negative. Therefore, the value of an option is always greater or equal to US$0.[18] On balance, the expected value next year is then: $50\% \times$ US$500 + $50\% \times$ US$0 = US$250. Discounted to today, this gives a value of US$250/(1 + 10%) = US$227. There is thus a considerable difference in value between the DCF and the real options approach. DCF assumes that once the investment is made, the decision cannot be reconsidered, whatever the market circumstances. DCF attributes no value to the flexibility of waiting a year or to the associated advantages. Real option valuation explicitly takes account of the fact that previous decisions (to invest or not?) can be changed if new information is released.

Valuation of a goldmine

One of the first applications of real options concerned the valuation of mines and oil fields (see, for example, Brennan and Schwartz, 1985). Suppose a company owns only one asset: the exploitation right on a goldmine. During a period of 20 years, 50,000 kilogrammes of gold can be brought to the surface per year. The price of gold is now US$400 per

---

[18] Readers who are familiar with option valuation will recognise 'value call = MAX (S – X, 0)'.

kilogramme and the operating costs are US$300 per kilogramme. Neither of these figures are expected to change. The standard deviation of the margin between the price of gold and the operating costs appears to be 20%, historically, and the risk-free rate is 7%. The non-recurring costs of making the mine operational for the extraction of the gold are US$50,000,000. The required return is 10%. What are the company's real options? The gold will only be extracted if the price is sufficiently higher than the costs (and covers the initial investment); the enterprise always has the option of closing the mine (if the prices decrease sharply or costs rise) and reopening it (if prices rise or costs decrease). Allowance should, however, be taken of the fact that closing the mine for one year entails a loss of 50,000 kilogrammes of gold which can never be recuperated because the exploitation right of the mine is limited in time.[19]

A DCF valuation results in a value of −US$7,432,181: US$42,567,819 (present value of 50,000 × (US$400−US$300) for a period of 20 years, discounted at 10%) − US$50,000,000, the required initial investment. However, if the value of the real options is taken into consideration – that is, the goldmine is only exploited if the future margin is large enough to recover the substantial initial investment (which will not be the case with the current margins), both the exploitation right and the company will have a value: by means of a Black and Scholes formula (adjusted for 'leakage'), a value of US$6,052,682 is found.

Valuation of an R&D project

In this section, an R&D project[20] is valued. Such projects typically show the following characteristics: there is first an initial phase of research that can later be followed by the development of the discovered product (in the case of success in the first phase and a favourable market). If this development is also successful and the market is still judged to be favourable, the product can be launched on the market.

Consider the following: the first phase of research into a new medicine requires US$1,500,000 and lasts one year.[21] The chance of success (based on the company's historical success ratios for similar projects) is 10% that it will be a very effective product, 10% of finding an average medicine and an 80% chance of no result at all. If a new medicine is discovered, phase 2 (the development) can be started,

---

[19] This leads to a 'leakage in value'; this is analogous to the effect of dividends on the value of the underlying share, and thus on the value of an option on this share.
[20] This example is greatly simplified: in reality there are for instance a lot more different phases, but the underlying idea remains the same.
[21] Cf. Copeland and Keenan (1998a, b).

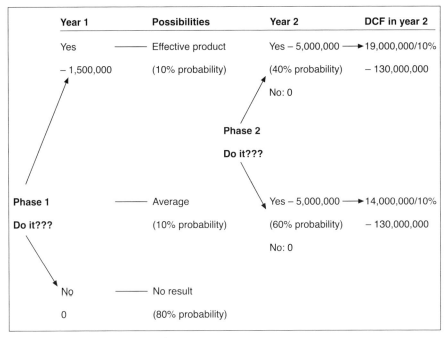

Figure 2.2   Decision tree.

which also takes a year. This phase costs US$5,000,000 and here too there are various possibilities: a 40% probability that the medicine will be approved after testing its effects on health, and a 60% probability that it will not be approved. If the medicine successfully withstands this phase, it can be introduced on the market. A very effective product generates an annual cash flow of US$19,000,000, and an average product US$14,000,000.[22] The total cost of establishing a production unit and putting the drugs on the market amounts to US$130,000,000. What is the value of this project?

Let us first present this project schematically on the basis of a decision tree (Figure 2.2). The value of this project according to the DCF method, which allows for these different scenarios and their respective probabilities, is –US$100,000. Real option valuation (the binomial model is most suitable here) results in a value of US$400,000. This extra value is obtained because the company is not obliged to start the development phase, even if a good medicine is found, and the company does not have to proceed with the introduction of the product if the cash flow forecasts deteriorate

---

[22] For the sake of simplicity, it is assumed that these cash flows are generated till infinity and that the discount rate is 10%.

over time, more than was initially expected. In these cases, value is created because the originally anticipated expenses for these steps can be avoided if the corresponding cash inflows are inadequate. On the other hand, these phases can be started if the market conditions are favourable. The company has the right to do this but is not obliged to do so. The right to do something (dynamic option approach) is always worth more than the obligation to do something (static DCF approach). The real options in this example are often present in pharmaceutical and biotechnology companies.

Valuation of a start-up

The following example is based on the illustration of valuation problems for a start-up studied by Amram and Kulatilaka (1999). What is the value of a newly established brewery, where US$4,000,000 (equally spread over each quarter) is needed for the first two years for product development and the start of production, and where the product can be launched on the market after two years if an additional US$12,000,000 is invested? It is expected that this supplementary investment will have a value at that moment (thus within two years) of US$22,000,000. The DCF method, again, assumes that all investments will be made, in spite of the option characteristics of the second investment.

The second investment opportunity is a growth option, a follow-up investment, and will depend upon the success of the first investment and the evolution in market circumstances. It concerns a European call option, with a duration of two years. The volatility of the project cash flows that can be obtained by exercising the growth option (an operational brewery) is estimated on the basis of the volatility of the share price of similar listed breweries. This results in a standard deviation estimate of 40%. A DCF analysis computes a negative value of US$230,000, assuming a risk-free interest rate of 5% and a required return of 21%, given the high risk profile. Real option valuation, in this case using Black and Scholes, produces a total positive value of US$1,130,000. The following parameters were used here: required investment for the follow-up investment (X) US$12,000,000; present value of expected cash flows of the follow-up investment (S) US$14,460,000; risk-free interest rate of 5% (r_f); time after which the follow-up investment can take place (t) 2 years; and a standard deviation (σ) of cash flows related to this investment of 40%. This results in a value of this option to make the follow-up investment of US$4,960,000. If the first required investment is taken into consideration, the value of the total company is equal to US$4,960,000 – present value of US$4,000,000 (this is US$500,000 each quarter during the first two years) = US$1,130,000. It is clear what causes this major difference in value: DCF assumes that whatever happens (also if the expected cash flows within two years are much lower than they are now forecasted), the follow-up investment will take place. The valuation of options explicitly states that the second investment will only be made if the value of the expected cash flows at that moment is higher than the required investment amount.

If account is also taken of the fact that the start-up company is able to stop the project each quarter (and thus avoid the remaining anticipated expenses; these are stopping options) if it appears that the launch of the product will never produce the desired cash flows after a particular period of time (new information is released all the time), then the total value of the start-up even increases to US$1,740,000.

4.8. Equity as a call option on the firm's assets

In a levered firm, equity is equivalent to a call option on the assets of the firm. The stockholders have the option to default on debt and debt holders will own the assets of the firm. By paying off debt, the stockholders acquire the firm's assets, free and clear. Therefore, the value of a firm's equity is like a (financial) call option on the firm's assets-in-place and its 'opportunities' (real options). The value of equity, from the call option perspective, will differ substantially from the standard valuation result in case of financial distress (value of debt close to firm value).

4.9. Critique of the real option method

Although conceptually superior to the traditional DCF method, the real option approach also has disadvantages. Firstly, the tracking of real options is unclear. Secondly, the valuation of real options is not obvious either.

Three aspects are involved here. First, the parameters that should be used as input for the option valuation model cannot always be adequately determined but have a major influence on the resulting valuation. A clear example is the expected volatility, which is very important for the determination of the value of the option, but which is difficult to estimate. A similar story applies to the duration of a real option: for example, how long can a company delay a project without the opportunity disappearing, because competitors take advantage of the situation? This parameter is also difficult to determine in most cases. Second, the use of the correct option valuation method. This is usually based on a number of underlying assumptions, which are not always true for real options and lead to distortions of the valuation. Third, a factor that does not make the valuation any easier is the underlying interaction of real options. Exercising a specific option frequently creates new options, while destroying others. This interaction should be kept in mind when determining the total value of the options; this is not simply the sum of the individual options.

Because of the above-mentioned complexity, and the fact that real options are a relatively new concept, this method is not yet often applied in practice. Nevertheless, this approach, which takes account of the flexibility of management and the value that arises because opportunities can be taken advantage of, is clearly preferable to the static DCF method that is too rigid in most situations and is based on unrealistic assumptions. Despite the complexity of real option models, it is better to be approximately correct and to estimate the value of these 'opportunities' as accurately as possible, than to be completely wrong by totally neglecting their value, as the DCF method does.

5. SUMMARY AND CONCLUSIONS

In this chapter an overview is provided of a number of important valuation methods. The DCF method is initially examined and the fundamental details discussed in order to correctly implement this method. A second valuation model is the APV method, which provides a clearer insight into exactly how value is created (operations versus financial side-effects) and avoids errors that easily occur in the DCF valuation using the WACC. However, both methods only succeed in valuing 'assets in place' and not the 'opportunities' that every company has. To this end, the real option approach must be used. In the future, this approach will be used more and more often, together with the APV method, rather than the traditional DCF valuation.[23]

It should be added to this that valuation is not an exact science and that a few important principles must be kept in mind. A company must be valued as a whole, allowing for all value affecting components. Real options add a lot of value to this because the possible opportunities for a company are evaluated and valued in addition to the existing assets and activities. Furthermore, it still holds that a valuation exercise is limited in time (value can change at any time, together with the economic and financial environment, an example being a change in the risk-free interest rate) and is very dependent upon what party performs the exercise. A potential buyer who, for example, can realise more synergies with a target will produce a higher valuation. And each potential

---

[23] Keuleneer (2000) emphasises the thinking about options in financial policy in general and for investment analysis and valuation in particular.

buyer has different options, thus the value will be different for each party involved.

REFERENCES

Amihud, Y., Mendelson, M., and Lauterbach, B., 'Market microstructure and securities values: evidence from the Tel Aviv Stock Exchange', *Journal of Financial Economics*, No. 45, 1997, 365–390.

Amram, M., and Kulatilaka, N., *Real Options: Managing Strategic Investment in an Uncertain World*, 1999, HBS Press, 246 pp.

Blanz, R., 'The relationship between return and the market value of common stocks', *Journal of Financial Economics*, March, 1981, 3–18.

Brennan, M., and Schwartz, E., 'Evaluating natural resource investments', *Journal of Business*, April, 1985, 135–157.

Brennan, M., and Tamarowski, C., 'Investor relations, liquidity and stock prices', *Journal of Applied Corporate Finance*, Vol. 12, No. 4, 2000.

Chen, N., Roll, R., and Ross, S., 'Economic forces and the stock market', *Journal of Business*, July, 1986, 303–404.

Copeland, T., and Antikarov, V., *Real Options: A Practitioner's Guide*, 2001, Texere, 372 pp.

Copeland, T., and Keenan, A., 'How much is flexibility worth?', *McKinsey Quarterly*, No. 2, 1998(a), 38–49.

Copeland, T., and Keenan, A., 'Making real options real?', *McKinsey Quarterly*, No. 3, 1998(b), 128–141.

Copeland, T., Koller, T., and Murrin, J., *Valuation: Measuring and Managing the Value of Companies*, 3rd edition, 2000, John Wiley & Sons, 494 pp.

Fama, E., and French, K., 'The cross-section of expected stock returns', *Journal of Finance*, June, 1992, 427–465.

Fama, E., and French, K., 'The equity premium', *Journal of Finance*, April, 2002, 637–659.

Keuleneer, L., *Options for Optimal Financial Management*, Inaugural lecture, 17/11/2000, Free University of Amsterdam.

Kothari, S., Shanken, J. and Sloan R., 'Another look at the cross-section of expected returns', *Journal of Finance*, December, 1995.

Luehrman, T., 'Using APV: A better tool for valuing operations', *Harvard Business Review*, May–June, 1997(a), 145–154.

Markowitz, H., *Portfolio Selection: Efficient Diversification of Investments*, Chapters 7 and 8, 1959, John Wiley & Sons.

Reinganum, M., 'Misspecification of capital asset pricing: empirical anomalies based on earnings yields and market values', *Journal of Financial Economics*, March, 1981, 19–46.

Reinganum, M., 'A revival of the small firm effect; far from being dead', *Journal of Portfolio Management*, Spring, 1992, 55–62.

Silber, W., 'Discounts on restricted stock: the impact of illiquidity on stock prices', *Financial Analysts Journal*, July–August, 1991, 60–64.

Smit, H., and Trigeorgis, L., 'Growth options, competition and strategy: an answer to the market valuation puzzle?', in *Real Options and Business Strategy: Applications in Decision Making*, 1992, Risk Books.

Van der Heijden, W., 'Is big beautiful?', *KPMG Corporate Finance*, March, 1999.

Chapter 3

Valuation in practice

Tom Copeland[1]

Professor Copeland has a PhD from the University of Pennsylvania and was a full-time professor at UCLA for 14 years. In addition, he was a partner of McKinsey & Co. for 11 years and has been a partner at Monitor Company for the past four years as Managing Director of its Corporate Finance Practice. He taught at the New York University and at MIT. Since 2002, he has lectured at Harvard University. Copeland is very well known for his book Financial Theory and Corporate Policy, *which is a standard work in many MBA programmes. He is also renowned for his books on valuation, particularly* Valuation: Measuring and Managing the Value of Companies, *the third edition of which was published at the end of 2000 and now includes an entire chapter devoted to the valuation of dot.coms. In 2001, he wrote a book on real options entitled* Real Options: A practitioner's guide.

1. INTRODUCTION

Changes in value are at the heart of economic decision-making. My work focuses on three elements of this: discounted cash flow valuation, expectations-based management and real options analysis. I would like to discuss how to value dot.coms or high-tech, high-growth companies, which involve some special challenges. I'll show you how we valued AOL before the Time Warner merger and Amazon.com at the same

---

[1]This chapter is based on a VERA presentation given by Tom Copeland in Amsterdam on 1 June 1999.

point in time and then again in January 2001. The only difference in the latter case was that in August 1999 Amazon.com was selling for US$100 a share and 18 months later it was selling for US$15 a share; that is quite a challenge for valuation. I will then talk about new research and insights into what I no longer call 'value-based management', but rather 'expectations-based management'. Finally, I will talk about real options for valuing projects, for thinking about strategy and for valuing companies.

2. DISCOUNTED CASH FLOW VALUATION

2.1. Introduction

The discounted cash flow model has been around for at least 100 years, but it wasn't used extensively until the mid-1980s and there is a reason for that. When I started teaching corporate finance at the graduate level in the late 1960s, we were still using slide rules and mechanical calculators for our calculations. It was rather difficult to teach extensive discounted cash flow spreadsheet analysis with a slide rule. At that point in time, only about 20% of companies were using net present value as a decision-making tool. Then in the 1970s pocket calculators were invented and that made it much easier to do the calculations. All of a sudden, net present value was used extensively by companies and, by the end of the 1970s, 85% of large companies were using net present value analysis as a technique for evaluating projects. In the 1980s, there was another innovation: computer spreadsheets appeared, first from a company called Lotus and subsequently Excel from Microsoft. But in any event, spreadsheets

---

Discounted Cash Flow Definition

DCF has three components:

Free Cash Flow = EBIT – Cash taxes on EBIT + Δ Accrued taxes due

+ Depreciation – Capital Expenditures

– Δ Operating working capital

$$\text{WACC} = K_b \,(1 - \text{marginal tax rate})\,\frac{B}{V} + K_S \frac{S}{V}$$

$$\text{Continuing Value} = \frac{\text{EBIT}(1 - \text{cash tax rate})(1 - g/r)}{\text{WACC} - g}$$

where g = NOPLAT growth and r = return on new investment made it quick and easier to calculate 10 years of income statements and balance sheets and cash flows and ratios. A professor at Northwestern University called Al Rappaport and his friend Carl Noble, a physicist, founded a company called Alcar and started selling spreadsheet models for US$3,000 a copy, and banks around the world were buying 50 copies each. It was a good business to be in and, of course, as it became a tool that people were using extensively, books started to appear on the subject. Tim Koller, Jack Murrin and I wrote a book called *Valuation: Measuring and Managing the Value of Companies*, that seemed to find the centre of the market and it became very popular. Most of the developments, however, were riding on the back of the work performed by Noble and Rappaport, with the underlying theory being based on the much earlier research by Modigliani and Miller. What has been happening during the past decade is that people are beginning to turn to real options. In a survey performed on 4,000 companies in the USA that was completed in 2001, Professor John Graham at Duke University asked the question: 'Has your company actually used real options for analysing decisions?' Of the respondents, 27% said they had. That really shocked me, because I would have guessed that no more than 5% would have tried it. So in 5 to 10 years from now, I expect that real options will be the dominant valuation paradigm. It won't make much difference in some situations and I'll describe what those situations are, but in other situations it will make a huge difference, and I'll describe what they are as well.

What is different about real options is that it requires the analysis of uncertainty. When you perform discounted cash flows, you are taking expected cash flows and discounting them at a risk-adjusted rate. The analysis of uncertainty gets swept under the table somewhat because the only place that you use it in the analysis is coming up with the cost of equity; there is a beta that you look up, which is basically a comparable. Monte Carlo simulations are a means of conducting this analysis. In the 1980s, Monte Carlo programmes were not so good, but in the 1990s two programmes, 'Crystal Ball' and 'At Risk', became easy enough to use for ordinary mortals to understand. It takes about an hour to learn how to use these programmes and they are capable of modelling time-series properties of, for example, mean reversion in cash flows, and they are capable of simultaneously modelling cross-sectional relationships, such as covariance among different types of cash flows. As the necessary tools for performing real options analysis have only now become available, it has taken nearly 30 years since the development of the Black and Scholes Financial Option model for real options to really take off.

By way of reminder, discounted cash flow has three components. There are expected cash flows, there's a discount rate and there's a continuing value number. The continuing value number usually accounts for more than 50% of the value of the company and people are pretty nervous about this because the continuing value starts in the eleventh year of the forecast. It's the value of the cash flows from year 11 on, at least in the 10-year forecasts that we make. Then there are empirical tests: do discounted cash flows work?

2.2. Empirical tests of discounted cash flow

In Figure 3.1, there are 35 large companies and the 31 survivors 11 years later. On the vertical axis you have the market value of the company divided by the book value, on the horizontal axis you have the discounted cash flow estimate of the value of the company using the discounted cash flow approach. The cross-sectional correlations are better than 90%. Also, the slope of the line is no different from one that the theory predicts it should be if it is an unbiased model and the intercept is not different from zero either, which is also what it predicts for an unbiased model. Figure 3.2 gives a sample of Japanese companies.

When you are valuing Japanese companies there are a few things to keep in mind, one being that many of them have under-utilised assets in the form of real estate. The rent on the real estate is not reflective of the value of the property and you have to know how much excess real estate that they have and include that in the valuation. Interestingly enough, for the average Japanese company at this time, which was after the bubble burst in Japan, only about 60%–70% of the value of the company was from operations, the rest was from cross-holdings of marketable securities and excess real estate.

Figure 3.3 is for a country that has some of the most creative accounting anywhere in the world: Italy. A journalist once asked me: 'Will the changes in international accounting standards change the valuation of companies?' My reply was that if it is the same information and it is just packaged differently there will not be any change at all. If the changes in regulations reveal new information, such as with the changes in the consolidation rules that took place in the early 1990s in Europe, then obviously the valuations will change. Even with creative accounting, cash is still cash.

Valuation works across industries as well (Figure 3.4). Banks and insurance companies again have high correlations. As long as the company is large and as long as there is good publicly available information about it then the match between discounted cash flow valuation and actual market value is pretty high. This even applies to robust growth companies (Figure 3.5).

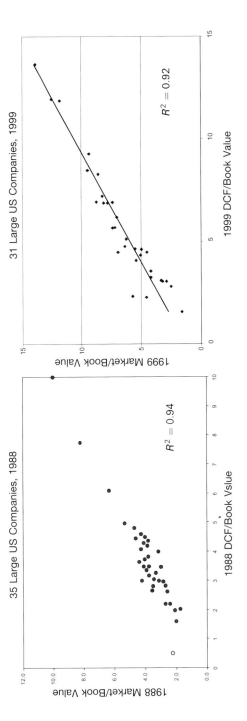

Figure 3.1 DCF works well for large publicly held companies. (*source* of left diagram: Value Line Forecasts; Copeland, Koller, Murrin, *Valuation*, 2nd edition, 1994; and of right diagram: Value Line Forecasts, Monitor Analysis).

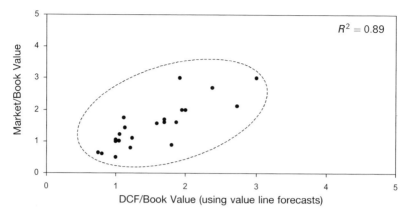

Figure 3.2 High correlation between market value and DCF value for 28 Japanese companies – 1993 (the R^2 for 28 Japanese companies was 89%). Comments: (1) under-utilised land and (2) cross-holdings.

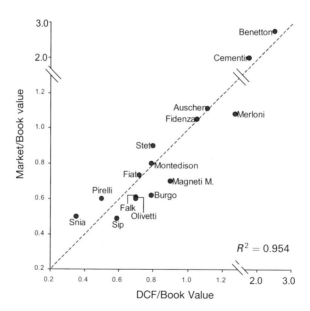

Figure 3.3 Correlation between DCF and market value – Italy (the R^2 for 15 Italian companies using publicly available information was 95.4%. This is based on the capitalisation on 28 September 1990 (Borsa valori di Milano), book value of company (*source*: Copeland, Koller and Murrin, *Valuation*). Comments: (1) Mark to market inflation accounting and (2) holder assets.

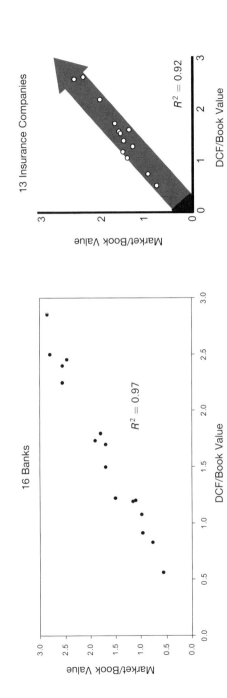

Figure 3.4 DCF works across different industries. *Note:* five banks are non-U.S. banks (*source:* Global Vantage: Value Line). Comments for left diagram: (1) equity approach and (2) income model/interest spread model. Comments for right diagram: (1) equity approach and (2) unrealised capital gains.

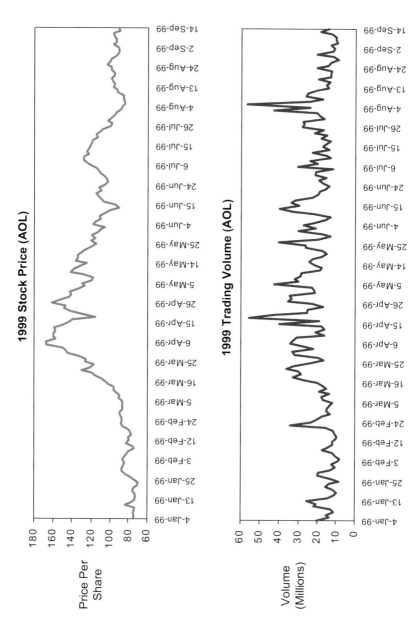

Figure 3.5 DCF works for robust growth companies. *Note:* 1999 elsewhere in valuation refers to FY 99 which ends in June (*source:* Compustat).

2.3. Discounted cash flow valuation of AOL

In August 1999, we valued AOL before the Time Warner merger as an example of a high-growth company. We used analysts' forecasts for the company's revenue growth. The analysts were predicting an average of 25% per year for the next five years. In the box at the bottom of Figure 3.6 you can see the year-by-year deviations between our forecasts and the average of the analysts forecast. The deviations are trivial.

In the next five years we cut the growth rate to 13.2% and then we cut it to 9% long-term, which I still think is rather aggressive, actually 6% or 7% would make me feel a little bit more comfortable. In order to value AOL you not only need to know its revenue growth, but you need to know how its business mixes are expected to change over time (Figure 3.7).

AOL is an Internet service provider. In 1999, 70% of the revenues came from online services and only 21% came from advertising. However, the growth rate in advertising is expected to be higher than the growth rate of online services and so consequently the business mix for the company will change substantially over time. Ten years from that point, in 2009, we were predicting that the revenues from advertising would nearly double as a percentage of the total pie. The important thing about this is that online services are predicted to become less and less profitable as prices

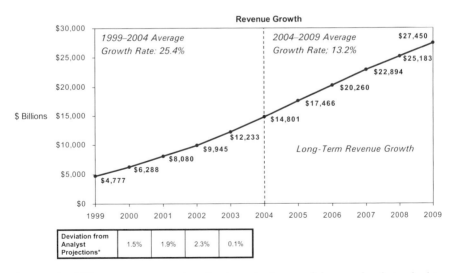

Figure 3.6 AOL revenue assumptions for the valuation model were closely tracked to analyst estimates of long-term revenue growth. *Most analysts did not forecast beyond 2003. *Note*: FY for AOL ends in June (*source*: INH Barings; BankBoston Robertson Stephens; Donaldson, Lufkin, and Jenrette).

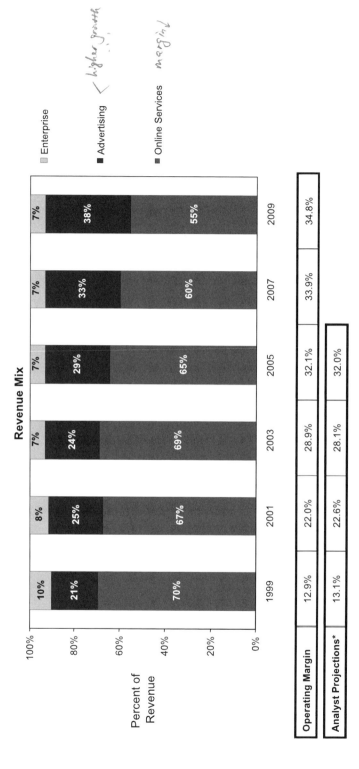

Figure 3.7 AOL projected operating margins benefit from both significant scale economies and changes in revenue mix toward higher margin businesses. *Average (*source:* ING Barings; BankBoston Robertson Stephens; Donaldson, Lufkin, and Jenrette).

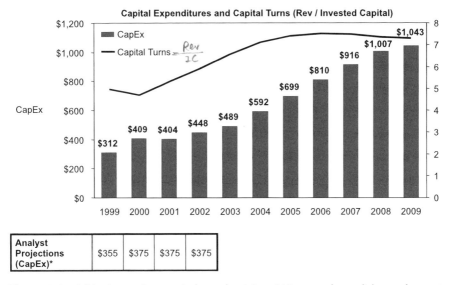

Analyst Projections (CapEx)*	$355	$375	$375	$375

Figure 3.8 AOL: increasing capital productivity. *Most analysts did not forecast beyond 2003 (*source*: ING Barings; BankBoston Robertson Stephens, Donaldson, Lufkin, and Jenrette).

decrease. Nevertheless, advertising services are actually pretty profitable on their own. So the leading Internet service providers were expected by the market at that time, and still are expected, to make much more of their profitability from the change in the business that they are likely to experience. Notice also that the operating margins that we pretty much assumed, were almost the same as the operating margins that the analysts were assuming. And the analysts were assuming an increase in operating margin due to the change in business mix.

Figure 3.8 shows capital expenditures and capital turns, which is revenue divided by invested capital, increasing and then stabilising over time.

When you put the financing of the company into the picture, a very, very important thing to consider is that AOL was still a risky company in 1999. Its growth rate is projected to be 25% for the next five years – plus or minus 10% on either side of that. Until the Internet service provider market shakes out, the variability is quite high. Therefore, the beta is 1.69 to 1.7. As the business mix changes and the company matures over time, we speculate that its beta will be a weighted average of a telecom company and a newspaper. Newspapers make their revenues primarily from advertising; telecom companies make their revenues primarily from subscriptions. The weighted average takes the equity beta down to 1.06. At

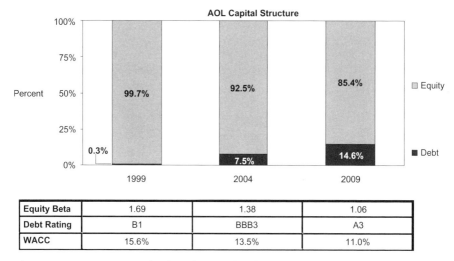

Equity Beta	1.69	1.38	1.06
Debt Rating	B1	BBB3	A3
WACC	15.6%	13.5%	11.0%

Figure 3.9 AOL maturing leads to the use of a changing WACC, based on comparables taken from telecom, software, and news media (*source*: Compustat, Bloomberg, Monitor Analysis).

the same time, I believe that as the size of the company increases and its cash flows become more stable, its ability to borrow debt goes up and also its credit rating would go up. So the weighted average cost to capital, which is shown in the bottom line of Figure 3.9, goes from 15.6% today down to 11% in 10 years from now.

When this is all put together, the long-term weighted average cost of capital is 11% and the rate of return on invested capital is 40%, the situation we expect in the tenth year. For the continuing value of the company, the question is whether it will continue to earn 40% return on invested capital. I think the answer is yes, unless regulation takes it away.

In Figure 3.10, you can see that a 40% return on invested capital and growth of 9% generates a continuing value estimate of US$84 billion, so the continuing value was about 70% of the total value of the company. But why would they earn 40% in long term? How do I defend that kind of assumption? Companies such as Intel and Coca-Cola have high rates of return because they have a competitive edge that is sustainable. For Coca-Cola it is their advertising expense and brand name that enable them to earn a 50% return, 40% the last few years, but still a lot, year after year. Why would that be true of AOL and other large Internet service providers? I think it is because of something called Metcalf's Law (Figure 3.11), which has to do with the number of interconnections or a measure of interconnectivity in a network.

Continuing Value		Return on New Investment		
		35%	40%	45%
NOPLAT Growth	8%	$55,933	$58,038	$59,674
	9%	$80,934	**$84,474**	$87,228
	10%	$155,025	$162,820	$168,883

WACC = 11% in the long run

Figure 3.10   AOL: continuing value. In the base case US$, continuing value contributes 85% of total operating value (approximately US$76 out of US$93 per share). Continuing value growth rate has a particularly large impact because the growth rate is very close to the ending WACC of 11%.

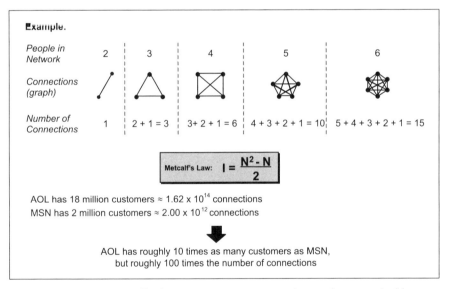

Figure 3.11   AOL: Metcalf's law (interconnectivity) makes scale a sustainable competitive advantage leading to perpetually high ROIC.

When you become a customer of an Internet service provider you want to be able to make connections quickly and easily to as many different things as you can. Metcalf's Law says that if there are two people in a network there is one connection, if there are three people three connections, four people six connections, five people 10, six people 15 connections and in general the number of connections in-creases as the square of the number of people in the network. So in the summer of 1999, AOL had 18 million customers and Microsoft network had 2 million customers, which looks like a ratio of roughly 10 to 1, but the economic power was more like 100 to 1, which is a significant difference. I predict that the Internet service provider industry will be oligopolistic in 10 years from now. In each major geography there will be two or three major players and a lot of minor players that don't make much difference. It is also assumed that the rates of return will be sustainable until reg-ulators decide to take these returns away.

All these assumptions produce a value of US$93 per share at a time when the trading range was between US$89 and US$104. We can debate endlessly about whether or not these assumptions are correct. The key assumptions for a high-growth company like this are, first of all, that the high growth will be slowing. Secondly, if different parts of the business are growing at different rates in a short space of time, the business mix will change significantly. Thirdly, the robust growth that is highly uncertain will become more certain over time and the risk of the company will go down so the discount rate is changing over time (Figure 3.12). Finally, an issue that is legitimately debatable, what will the long-term rate of return on invested capital be relative to the cost of capital?

One of the things that come out of a discounted cash flow model is a price earnings ratio or a market to book ratio, which is price over book value shown in the lower line in Figure 3.13.

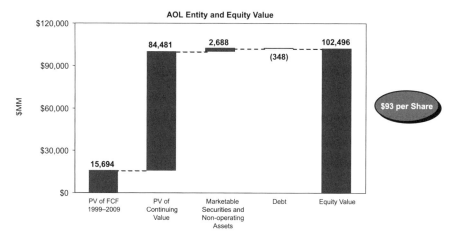

Figure 3.12   AOL: the changing WACC and continuing value assumptions bridge the analyst projections and the current market value (implied share price of US$93 versus trading range of US$89 to US$104 between mid-August and mid-September).

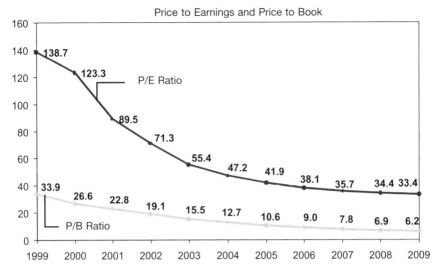

Figure 3.13   AOL market ratios decline over time as the firm matures.

At the time we were doing the valuation, the price earnings ratio for AOL was 140 times earnings. That is not unusual for a company that has both positive earnings and is growing very rapidly, but that ratio is not appropriate to use in any continuing value estimate because the company is going to be quite different in 10 years from now. So you cannot take 140 and plug it into earnings 10 years from now and get a valuation that is any way near to reality. But if you reverse engineer it, you can say if I take the assumptions of a discounted cash flow model, the continuing value or the terminal value is an estimate of the value 10 years from now. If I take that entity value and subtract the amount of debt and divide by the earnings at that point in time, the model forecasts the price earnings ratio in 10 years time. This was 33 in 1999 when the average price earnings ratio was about 25, so the assumptions do not sound so unreasonable when you look at it in that context.

$$P/E = \frac{V_E - V_D}{EPS}$$

2.4. Discounted cash flow valuation of Amazon.com

Amazon.com is another company that people have talked about and are still talking about because of its remarkable ability to generate losses and yet retain a high valuation (Figure 3.14). In August 1999, Amazon.com

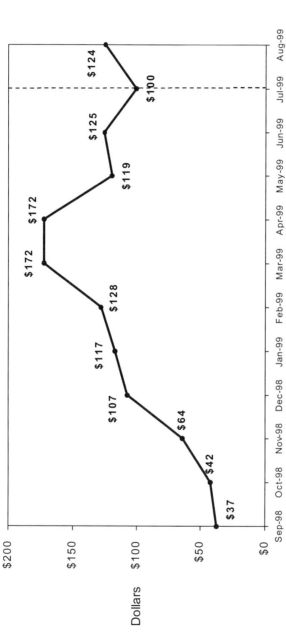

Figure 3.14 Amazon.com: Amazon's stock (up to August 1999). On 12 August 1999 Amazon.com undertook a 2 for 1 stock split. As our valuation reflects the value of the company in July 1999 we will use the number of outstanding shares before the split.

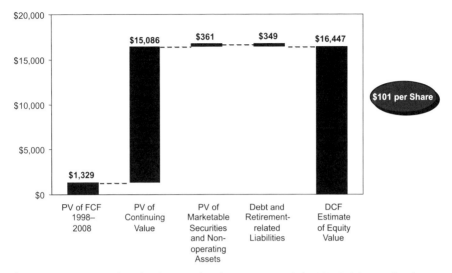

Figure 3.15 Monitor's valuation results: Amazon.com (July 1999). *Note*: valuation as of July 1999 reflects pre-split price of US$101/share. Trading range was US$126.50 to US$97.50.

was selling for roughly US$100 a share and it had never made positive earnings, and it wasn't expected to make positive earnings for several years.

How do you explain the value of a company like that? The interesting thing is that Amazon.com has negative working capital. The faster the company grows the more cash they generate, and the reason they have negative capital is that you pay them for the books before they pay for the books they order from their supplier, so when they are growing fast they generate cash (Figure 3.15). *Reader's Digest* magazines are another example of this; when the growth slows they stop generating cash. Therefore, although they are negative in terms of earnings, they are positive in terms of cash flow even now, even though not so much today as in August 1999. In any event, at the beginning of August 1999 our valuation turned out at US$101 per share. The continuing value was US$15 billion, the present value of cash flows for the next 10 years was US$1.3 billion, so you can imagine there might be high variability in the stock price.

In Figure 3.16 you can see the operating assumptions that we used: revenue growth 50% the first year, 39% the second year, declining to 21% over the 10-year period. Figure 3.16 also shows the cost of goods sold, selling, general and administrative expenses, and capital expenditures as a percentage of revenue. Please note that the net working capital/revenue percentages are all negative.

	Monitor
Revenue Growth	2000 – 50% 2001 – 39.2% 2002 onward 39.2% declining to 21%
COGS / Revenue	2000 – 77% 2001 – 76% 2002 – 74%
SG&A / Revenue	2000 – 28% 2001 – 22.4% 2002 – 15% declining to 10.5%
Capex / Revenue	2000 – 2% 2001 – 1.5% 2002 – 1.5%
Net Working Capital / Revenue	2000 – -16% 2001 – -17.5% 2002 – -17.5%

Figure 3.16 Summary operating assumptions July 1999.

Where revenue growth assumptions are concerned, the analysts at that time were saying 40% per year for the next five years and we had roughly half of that for the next five years thereafter and 9% in the long term. The weighted average cost of capital was also high and declining and it declined to 10% long term. The interesting thing is that the return on net new investment long term was 11% for Amazon.com (Figure 3.17). We could not think of any sustainable competitive advantage that they had other than brand name.

Since 1999, the fortunes of Amazon have changed. It split two for one and the price fell from its peak down to US$15 a share in January 2001 representing a 70% decrease in the share price. How can we use the same model to explain this? The answer is that the model didn't change, but rather the analysts' expectations that were revised dramatically. If you do the value build-up in July 1999 you get US$101 per share, but if you do the value build-up again using different information and different analysts' forecasts you get US$15.30 a share in January 2001 (Figure 3.18). The last two columns of Figure 3.19 show the consensus assumptions that we used on the two dates. The most important assumptions are revenue growth declining from 39.2% to 21% in the model that we did in July 1999 (Figure 3.20) while the analysts' consensus was 29% declining to 17%.

Continuing Value Sensitivity		Return on New Investment		
		10%	11%	12%
NOPLAT Growth	9%	$66	**$102**	$132
	8%	$66	$82	$95
	7%	$66	$75	$83

WACC = 10% in the long run

Figure 3.17 Amazon.com: sensitivity analysis of price per share. Ninety-two per cent of Amazon's market value is realised after the year 2009 and is reflected in the continuous value. The assumptions about the two parameters of Amazon's continuous value, NOPLAT growth and return on new investment are key to its valuation.

Discounted cash flow valuation does seem to work well for large companies even when they show robust growth like Amazon.com and AOL.

3. EXPECTATIONS-BASED MANAGEMENT

3.1. Company performance measurement

I would now like to link the changes in the values of companies to performance measurement of the companies internally and externally, which is what I call 'expectations-based management'. This is an important topic for me as a consultant because CEOs and CFOs are always concerned about how they establish performance standards for the people that work for them and how they can link these performance standards to what they observe in the stock market.

Figure 3.21 shows traditional measures like sales growth, earnings per share or earnings per share growth, together with their shortcomings. Sales growth ignores both balance sheet and income statement information. The next two, earnings per share and earnings per share growth, completely ignore balance sheet information. Return on invested capital, or the difference between the return on invested capital and the weighted average cost of capital, encourages harvesting behaviour. If you say to your managers that you want a higher return on invested capital they stop investing and the return (EBIT) stays the same and invested capital goes down because of depreciation, so the easiest way to make

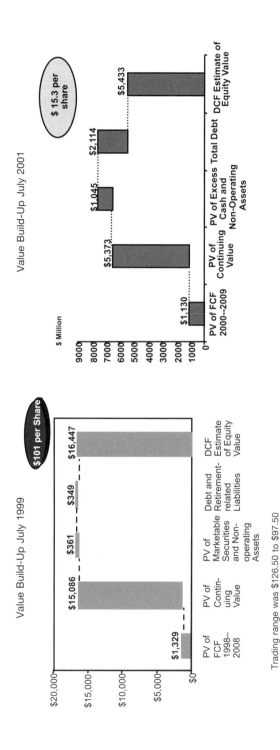

Figure 3.18 Amazon.com: valuation results July 1999 vs. January 2001. *Note*: Valuation as of July 1999 reflects pre-split price of $101/share. Trading range was $126.50 to $97.50.

	1997 – 1999 History	Jefferies	Merrill Lynch	Bernstein	Robertson Stephens	Monitor January '01	Monitor July '99
Revenue Growth	Avg 440%	2000 – 70.5% 2001 – 43.1% 2002 – 38.7%	2000 – 67.7% 2001 – 29.2%	2000 – 67.7% 2001 – 35% 2002 – 20%	2000 – 67.7% 2001 – 36.4% 2002 – 30%	2000 – 68.7% ↑ 2001 – 38.2% ↓ 2002 onward 29.6% declining to 17.5% ↓	2000 – 50% 2001 – 39.2% 2002 onward 39.2% declining to 21%
COGS / Revenue	Avg 78.2% 1998 – 76.5% 1999 – 80%	2000 – 74% 2001 – 74.2% 2002 – 73.8%	2000 – 75.2% 2001 – 75%	2000 – 75.2% 2001 – 75.5%	2000 – 75.2% 2001 – 76% 2002 – 74.1%	2000 – 74.5% ↓ 2001 – 74.9% ↓ 2002 – 73.6%	2000 – 77% 2001 – 76% 2002 – 74%
SG&A / Revenue	Avg 37.5% 1998 – 32.1% 1999 – 41.1%	2000 – 37.4% 2001 – 29% 2002 – 23.3%	2000 – 35.1% 2001 – 27.2%	2000 – 35.1% 2001 – 29.2%	2000 – 35.1% 2001 – 27.5% 2002 – 23.5%	2000 – 35.6% ↑ 2001 – 28.2% ↑ 2002 – 23.4% declining to 20.2% ↑	2000 – 28% 2001 – 22.4% 2002 – 15% declining to 10.5%
Capex / Revenue	Avg 10.1% 1998 – 5% 1999 – 19.8%	2000 – 4.5% 2001 – 3.1% 2002 – 2.3%		2000 – 10.3% 2001 – 1.6% 2002 – 0.9%		2000 – 7.4% ↑ 2001 – 2.4% ↑ 2002 – 1.6%	2000 – 2% 2001 – 1.5% 2002 – 1.5%
Net Working Capital / Revenue	Avg – –19.3% 1998 – –16% 1999 – –23.5%	2000 – –18.8% 2001 – –12.5% 2002 – –13.2%				2000 – –16.8% 2001 – –10.5% ↑ 2002 – –12.7% ↑	2000 – –16% 2001 – –17.5% 2002 – –17.5%

Figure 3.19   Amazon.com: operating assumptions.

	Monitor Assumptions January 2001	Monitor Assumptions July 1999
WACC		
Barra Beta	2.09	1.91
Risk Free Rate	5.3%	6.3%
Credit Rating	B	B
Pre-tax Cost of Debt	10.9% (Debt / Total Capital (market value) 21.7%)	11.8% (Debt / Total Capital (market value) 2.1%)
Cost of Equity	16.8% (Equity / Total Capital (market value) 78.3%)	16.8% (Equity / Total Capital (market value) 97.9%)
WACC	14.5% declining to 10% by 2009	16.6% declining to 10% by 2009
Continuing Value		
Growth in NOPLAT	9%	9%
Return on Net New Investments	11%	11%

Figure 3.20   Amazon.com: WACC and continuing value assumptions.

Metric	Critique
Sales Growth	Ignores profitability, ignores balance sheet
EPS	Ignores balance sheet
EPS Growth	Ignores balance sheet
ROIC = EBIT/Invested Capital	Encourages harvesting behaviour
ROIC − WACC	Encourages harvesting
EVA $^{\textcircled{R}}$ = (ROIC − WACC) × Invested Capital	Not correlated with TRS
Rational Expectations	Best of short-term metrics

Figure 3.21   An example: performance measurement. Most traditional performance metrics create perverse incentives to management. Only rational expectations focus on shareholder value creation.   *TRS Total shareholder Return*

the target is to harvest the business. EVA® has been used by a lot of companies. It is measured as the difference between the return on invested capital and the cost of capital multiplied by the amount of invested capital. Unfortunately, it is not correlated with the total return to shareholders. So I'm going to talk about rational expectations, which brings the market's expectations into the picture, and show you that the correlation is almost 50% cross-sectionally.

3.2. Expectations-based management: examples

3.2.1. Sears vs. Wal-Mart

In Figures 3.22 and 3.23 you can see a comparison between Sears and Wal-Mart over a period of four years, which is quite a long time in the history of a company. Sales revenue growth for Sears is negative 9% on average, while the revenue growth for Wal-Mart is positive 13% on average, so Wal-Mart did better on sales revenue growth. Sears' net income was flat, thus no growth. Wal-Mart grew at 10% per year, so in terms of growth of the bottom line Wal-Mart did better. In terms of capital usage, the amount of capital used at Sears grew by 16.5% per year and only grew by 7% per year at Wal-Mart. So Wal-Mart grew and used capital more efficiently and was therefore doing better than Sears. If you look at economic profit, which is also EVA®, Wal-Mart did better as well, so everyone who has ever looked at this chart reaches the same conclusion.

	Sears*					Wal-Mart				
	1994	1995	1996	1997	CAGR	1994	1995	1996	1997	CAGR
Sales Revenue (billions)	$54.6	$34.9	$38.2	$41.3	-8.9%	$82.5	$93.6	$104.9	$118.0	12.7%
EBIT (billions)	$3.4	$3.1	$3.5	$3.9	4.7%	$3.6	$4.1	$4.1	$4.4	6.9%
Net Income (billions)**	$1.2	$1.0	$1.3	$1.2	0.0%	$2.6	$2.7	$3.1	$3.5	10.4%
ROIC	19.5%	-5.3%	-4.2%	-5.2%	—	10.4%	8.9%	8.9%	9.8%	—
WACC	9.1%	7.3%	8.1%	7.5%	—	12.5%	10.0%	11.0%	10.6%	—
ROIC–WACC	10.4%	-12.6%	-12.3%	-12.7%	—	-2.1%	-1.1%	-2.1%	-0.8%	—
Invested Capital (billions)	$21.66	$28.20	$30.19	$34.22	16.5%	$29.84	$33.54	$34.56	$36.60	7.0%
Economic Profit (billions) EVA	$2.24	-$3.56	-$3.72	-$4.33	—	-$0.63	-$0.36	-$0.73	-$0.28	—
Change in EP (billions)		-5.80	-0.16	-0.61	—		0.27	-0.37	0.45	—

* Excludes Allstate
** Before extraordinary items

Figure 3.22 Which company did better? Sears vs. Wal-Mart. A good example is found in the comparison between Wal-Mart and Sears over the 1994–1997 four-year interval. Can you tell from the data above which company had superior total return to shareholders? Sears 'destroyed' on aggregate of US$9.37 billion while Wal-Mart 'destroyed' US$2.00 billion.

Measured in terms of standard financial performance, Wal-Mart did better than Sears, there's no question about that. However, there is another measure of performance, the one that the boardroom looks at, and that is what happened to the stock price.

The total return to shareholders for Sears is the top line. Sears had over a 100% return to shareholders, Wal-Mart had about a 35% return. The explanation for this is that stock prices reflect expectations of future performance. The stock price for Wal-Mart was high at the beginning of this time period because the market expected Wal-Mart to do extremely well, and it did, but slightly less well than expected and, although the total return to shareholders was positive, it wasn't great. Sears on the other hand was expected to do poorly and it did, but it did better than expected and so its stock price went up over 100%.

Interestingly enough, this brings the subjective nature of performance back into the picture. EVA® was an attempt to make everything objective, the return on invested capital can be measured objectively, the weighted average cost of capital can be measured objectively, but neither of these contain information about expectations. The market works on expectations. I have a few quotes about Sears that are consistent with this point of

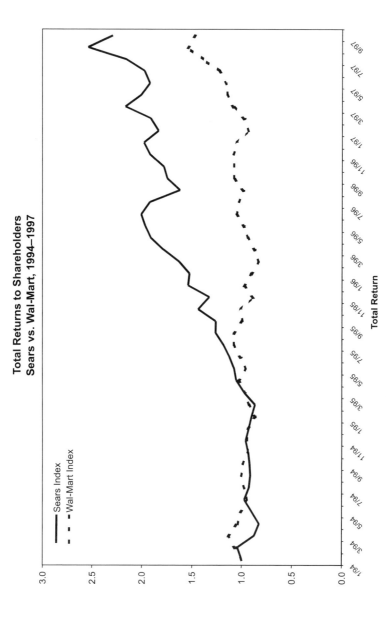

Figure 3.23   Between January 1994 and December 1997 the total return to shareholders of Sears was consistently higher than the total return to shareholders of Wal-Mart.

view: 'The better than expected results prompted several analysts to raise their Sears earnings forecast.' For Wal-Mart: 'The gap between expected and reported earnings has narrowed. Analysts had expected Wal-Mart to perform a bit better.'

3.2.2. Chevron

Figure 3.24 also illustrates how changes in analysts' expectations match total shareholder return for another company, Chevron. The 1993 box and the 1995 box are actual earnings that went from about US$2.50 to roughly US$3.00 a share. The stock price, represented by the top line, fell the whole year.

The key line here is the squiggly line between the two above-mentioned boxes, which is a measure of consensus analyst forecasts starting two years earlier. Two years earlier, the analysts were expecting that Chevron would deliver US$3.50 in 1995 and they constantly had to revise their expectations downward as they got closer to the actual date until Chevron finally delivered US$3 billion instead of US$3.50. The stock price went down because Chevron disappointed the expectations that had been set earlier.

3.2.3. Coca-Cola

Another example is the Coca-Cola company for the period 1995–98. It experienced outstanding growth and earnings during most of this period: US$1.18 in 1995, US$1.41 a year later and US$1.67 in 1997, while the expectation for 1998 was US$1.95. If I cover up the top line, analysts' expectations as early as two years before the actual earnings event were spot on. At the beginning of 1995 or the end of 1994, the prediction was US$1.40 a share and two years later it was US$1.41.

If a company is meeting expectations exactly, you would expect that the total return to shareholders would go up just like the cost of equity, that is, by about 14%–15% per year. The interesting year is when the Asian crisis hit (Figure 3.25) and the Indonesian rupiah fell 70% against the US dollar and the Korean won fell 40%. A can of Coca-Cola became a luxury good in those countries. When that happened the analysts did not revise their one-year ahead forecasts very much. The longer term forecasts, including the two-year ahead forecast, were knocked down tremendously. They had been expecting US$1.95 from Coca-Cola, but by the end of 1997 they were predicting US$1.70 (Figure 3.26).

What this shows is that if you have information about earnings you cannot predict what is going to happen to the stock price. Similarly, if you have information about the change in earnings you cannot predict either.

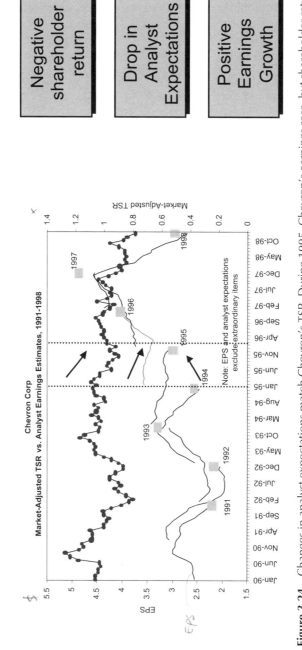

Figure 3.24 Changes in analyst expectations match Chevron's TSR. During 1995, Chevron's earnings rose, but shareholder return was negative. Why? Because during the year market expectations declined.

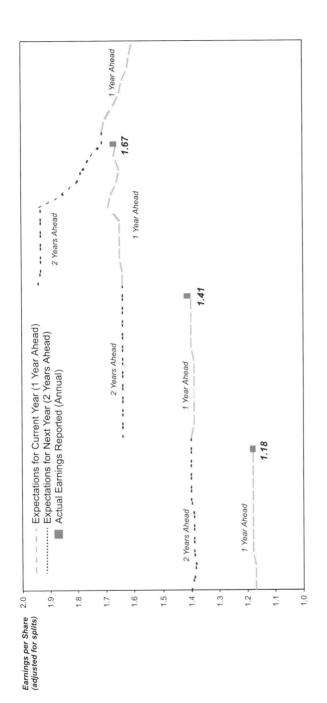

Figure 3.25 Analyst expectations of Coca-Cola EPS, 1995–1998: the Asian crisis. Analyst's expectations of Coca-Cola remained fairly constant during 1995 and 1996. However, falling expectations during 1997 and 1998 resulted in below market stock performance (*source*: IBES, Monitor Analysis).

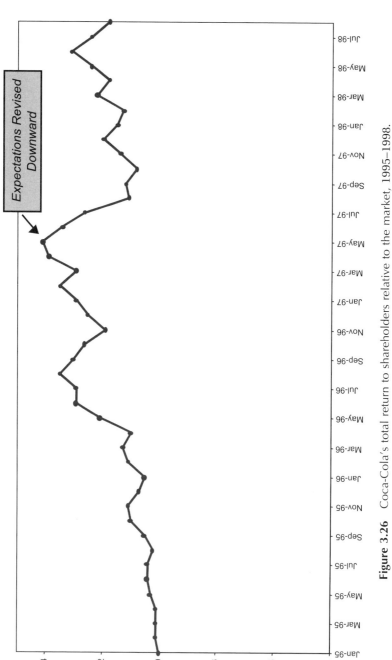

Figure 3.26 Coca-Cola's total return to shareholders relative to the market, 1995–1998.

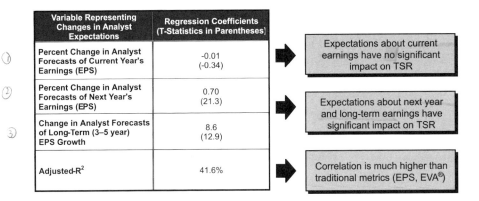

Variable Representing Changes in Analyst Expectations	Regression Coefficients (T-Statistics in Parentheses)
Percent Change in Analyst Forecasts of Current Year's Earnings (EPS)	-0.01 (-0.34)
Percent Change in Analyst Forecasts of Next Year's Earnings (EPS)	0.70 (21.3)
Change in Analyst Forecasts of Long-Term (3–5 year) EPS Growth	8.6 (12.9)
Adjusted-R^2	41.6%

Expectations about current earnings have no significant impact on TSR

Expectations about next year and long-term earnings have significant impact on TSR

Correlation is much higher than traditional metrics (EPS, EVA®)

Figure 3.27 Multiple regression results. Multiple regressions of market-adjusted total shareholder return (TSR) vs. changes in analyst earnings (EPS) expectations indicate a strong correlation between expectations and returns. Results of S&P 500 firms during 1992–98. Sample has 2,390 observations.

However, if you have information about changes in analysts' expectations you are able to predict.

3.3. Expectations and total shareholder return

Multiple regressions of market-adjusted total shareholder return versus changes in analyst earnings expectations indicate a strong correlation between expectations and returns. In the example shown in Figure 3.27, the overall correlation is almost 42%. Three variables are used, all of them covering changes in expectations this year. The first variable is the change in expectations this year about this year's earnings. The coefficient to zero is not significant. The second variable is changes in expectations this year about next year's earnings. The coefficient is significant at a level so high that it is not even worth writing down. The number in parentheses is a *t*-statistic. If it is greater than 1.96, you pass the 5% confidence level in a two-tail test. In this case it is more than 10 times higher, so the level of significance is virtually 100%. The coefficient is 0.7. The next variable shows changes in expectations this year about long-term earnings. This is also highly significant. The *t*-test is 13 and the coefficient is 8.6. What this tells you is that most of the information which the market actually responds to is information about the long-term prospects of the company.

3.4. Expectations-based management: an integrated framework

What I'm really saying is that expectations-based management takes EVA® and looks at the difference between expected EVA® and actual

> **Value-Based Management**
>
> $$\text{Economic Profit} = (\text{ROIC} - \text{WACC}) \times \text{Invested Capital}$$
>
> **Expectations-Based Management:**
>
> $\Delta\text{EP} = [\text{Actual ROIC} - \text{Expected ROIC}] \times \text{Invested Capital} \rightarrow \text{Work Core Assets Harder}$
>
> $\quad - [\text{Actual WACC} - \text{Expected WACC}] \times \text{Invested Capital} \rightarrow \text{Lower Cost of Capital}$
>
> $\quad + [\text{ROIC} - \text{WACC}] \times [\text{Actual IC} - \text{Expected IC}] \rightarrow \text{Invest Profitably}$

Figure 3.28   The complete picture.

EVA®. In Figure 3.28, I have called that the delta, the change in EVA® in economic profit, on the left-hand side of the second equation. You take the first term which is ROIC and you break it down into the difference between the actual return on invested capital and the expected return in invested capital times the amount of the invested capital, weighted average cost of capital drops out of the equation because it's a constant in the first term. The second term is the difference between the actual and expected weighted average cost of capital times the amount of invested capital and the third term is ROIC minus WACC times the difference between actual and expected investment. Each of these terms has a very natural interpretation. The first term says take the invested capital that is currently in place, the core capital, and work it harder; earn more than expected. That is how you create value. The second term says that if your financial officer can reduce your cost of capital below what was expected, that will also create value. The third term says that if you invest more than the market expects and you do so profitably, earning a positive return over your cost of capital, that will also create value. It is essential to invest profitably and not merely invest because, if the return on invested capital is less than the weighted average cost of capital, you destroy value (Figure 3.29).

4. REAL OPTIONS

4.1. Introduction

This is the single most important idea in corporate finance in 30 years as far as I'm concerned. A real option, like a financial option, is simply the right to do something for a predetermined price for a predetermined period of time. The words are important here; it is the right to do something, not the obligation, so if you have a real option you don't have to take the action (Figure 3.30).

The difference between a real option and a bet is that if you take a bet

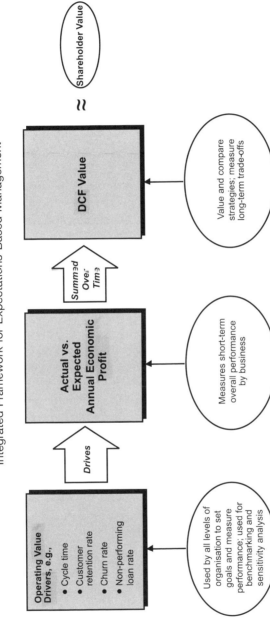

Figure 3.29 EBM. Together, DCF, EP, and value drivers form an integrated framework for value creation. DCF is comprehensive, long-term based, EP is a comprehensive, short-term measure, and value drivers are specific, short-term measures.

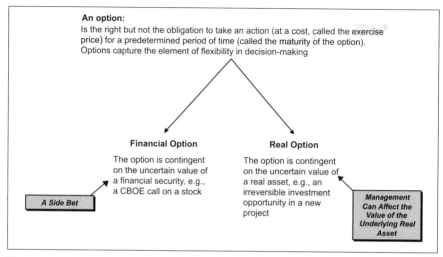

Figure 3.30   An option – definition. In environments with high uncertainty and room for managerial flexibility, investments will have considerable option (strategic) value, which needs to be considered.

you win or you lose for sure. If you take a real option and the uncertainty is resolved in your favour you win and if it's resolved against you simply don't take the action. Therefore, the payouts on real options with financial options are asymmetric. Scholars have found examples of real options throughout the literature of mankind. The earliest example was in the writings of Aristotle around 200 BC where he tells the story of a philosopher named Thales who lived on Milos in the Mediterranean. Thales read the tea leaves which predicted a very bountiful olive harvest that year. So Thales took his meagre life savings and went to the people who owned the olive presses and said: 'I'll give you all my savings if you give me the right to rent the presses at the normal rental rates during the harvest season.' They applied their expected cash flow models to this and they said: 'We will get our expected cash flow for sure and he's paying us something extra for that so we'll take his money.' When they did that, Thales acquired a 'real option'. The underlying risky asset in this case is the rental value of the presses. If the rental value of the presses is higher than the normal rental price, he'll pay the normal rental price to the owner and he'll receive the market value and make money. If the market rental value is lower he won't exercise his option. The exercise price, which is sometimes called the striking price, is the fixed price at which you can take the action; that is, the normal rental value. The life of the option is the time to harvest and the value he paid for the option is his life savings. He didn't have the benefit of the Black and Scholes formulas or stochastic differential calculus to solve the problem but Thales solved it in his head in the year 200 BC.

Now you can find examples of real options everywhere and as I go through this subject what I'm going to do mostly is paint examples, lots of examples, of real options. Now by way of contrast is your looking at a project. What you learn at university is that you take the expected cash flows on the project for the life of the project, you discount them at the weighted average cost of capital, then you subtract the initial investment. The resulting number is called the net present value; if it's negative you are not supposed to take the project, and yet senior managers take negative net present value projects all the time for strategic reasons. The arguments outlined above have to be in the game. Or if we don't do this we'll be worse off. Or we have to grow at any cost. Sometimes they are ridiculed for that wisdom, but it turns out there is truth behind it. What they are saying is that the word 'to manage' means to make decisions in the future and they know that they can manage the project. If the project turns out to be successful they will put more money into it and expand it or extend its life. If it turns out to be unsuccessful they will scale it down or they will abandon it all together. If it turns out to be highly risky today they may just decide to defer the start of the project until next year. So I have just mentioned five types of flexibility, ①expansion, ②extension, ③contraction, ④abandonment and ⑤deferral that every project has. None of which are taken into account using that present value analysis. So I have come to the conclusion after spending a long time thinking about this that net present value analysis, which is the standard paradigm in decision-making, systematically undervalues every project. It is only a question of how much.

Now projects that are so-called 'deep in-the-money' – what deep in the money means is that they have a very high net present value – don't need flexibility and so with projects that are very high in net present value you simply just go as fast and as furious as you can with them. You really don't need any flexibility in decision-making. Projects which are very low net present value are deep out-of-the-money options and the value of flexibility is very low in that case as well. It's the ones in the middle, the ones that the boardroom struggles over, which are nearer the money options because their net present value is anywhere from plus or minus 10% of the total amount being invested. In those cases the real options answers will be 100%, 200%, 300% different than the net present value analysis, and thank goodness for consultants because those are the ones that management are struggling over and we can come in and help out.

The first problem that you have when you are confronted with a real option is recognising it. Take the following example (Figure 3.31). There's

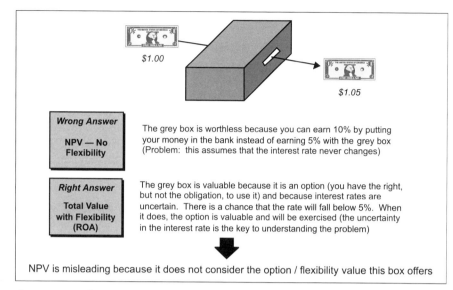

$1.00

$1.05

Wrong Answer	
NPV — No Flexibility	The grey box is worthless because you can earn 10% by putting your money in the bank instead of earning 5% with the grey box (Problem: this assumes that the interest rate never changes)

Right Answer	
Total Value with Flexibility (ROA)	The grey box is valuable because it is an option (you have the right, but not the obligation, to use it) and because interest rates are uncertain. There is a chance that the rate will fall below 5%. When it does, the option is valuable and will be exercised (the uncertainty in the interest rate is the key to understanding the problem)

NPV is misleading because it does not consider the option / flexibility value this box offers

Figure 3.31 Identifying options – an example of a simple option. Consider a situation where you can put US$1.00 into a grey box and get US$1.05 back after a year with absolute certainty. Current interest rates are 10%. How much is the grey box worth? (*source*: Steve Ross, Sterling Professor of Economics and Finance at Yale University)

a grey box into which you can put one dollar at any time during the next year. One year from the day you put the dollar into the grey box you receive one dollar and five cents with absolute certainty. If the interest rate at the bank is currently 10%, how much is the grey box worth? At first sight, if you put the money in the bank you get 10%, but if you put your money in the box you only get 5% so the box is worth nothing and the opportunity cost is 10%. However, interest rates are variable and if there is a finite probability that that interest rate goes to lower than 5% at any time during the next year, the box is worth something. In fact, the box is a call option on interest rates, it is a real option.

What are the classes of problems where real options make a big difference? Any [1] research and development programme is a real option, [2] any multiphase investment programme, like building a plant, is a real option, [3] any activity that you can start up and shut down is a real option, [4] any exploration and production decision is a real option, any [5] merger and acquisition programme is a real option, [6] any capital expenditure over a period of time is a real option.

One of the obstacles to the use of real options is that, up until fairly recently, you had to know eta-calculus stochastic differential equations to solve these problems in closed forms and that is why many of the experts working in the City or Wall Street are mathematicians or physicists rather than economists. But the economists are finally catching up and the book that I wrote on real options requires nothing more than algebra and knowledge of Excel spreadsheets to solve complex problems.

4.2. Coal lease valuation

I would like to give you a few examples of using real options. The first is an American call (Figure 3.32). A company was bidding on the right to develop a coal lease in Australia. Just like offshore oil leases this lease was exploitable for a five-year period and if you did not start to develop the property in five years, you know that by spending hundreds of millions of dollars, the lease would revert to the government. But for five years you had the monopoly right to decide to develop the property and decide to extract the coal.

One of the tricky things about this particular coal lease was that the extraction costs per tonne were fairly high. These costs were in fact US$1 below the revenue per tonne of coal, which meant that profits doubled if the revenue per ton of coal increased by a dollar and that there were no

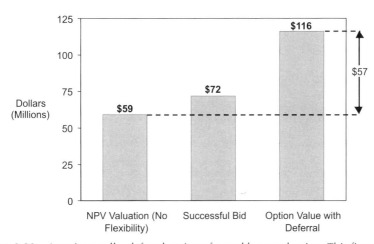

Figure 3.32 American call – deferral option of a coal lease valuation. This first example is a simple deferral option on the development of a coal lease for up to five years after the lease was acquired. *Comments*: (1) single source of uncertainly – price of coal; (2) NPV approach ignored flexibility; (3) option was particularly valuable because it was 'near-the-money', in other words the price of coal was close to the cost of extraction (options on deep in-the-money situations are not worth much because you invest immediately).

profits if the revenue went down by a dollar. The real price of coal was growing and it was extrapolated through time; the extraction costs were estimated and subtracted. The free cash flows were then discounted at the cost of capital and the initial investment was subtracted. That produced the value of about US$16 million, but rumour had it that the winning bid was going to be higher than that and the company could not figure out why until they realised that there is a deferral option involved here. You don't have to develop the mine immediately, you can wait a year and see whether the price of coal is higher or lower and if it gets high enough it will pay for the cost of developing the property and if it doesn't get high enough you lose the amount of money you paid to acquire the lease. So when they looked at it as a deferral option, the additional value was about the same as the original value and they ended up paying US$72 million and got lucky. Due to increases in the price of coal, this property was worth about US$800 million in the mid-1990s.

4.3. Cancellable operating lease valuation

The next example is probably my favourite. It concerns work that was done in 1990 for a manufacturer of jet engines. If you count the Russians and Chinese, there are only about five jet engine manufacturers in the world, but in spite of that the competition to get engines onto the wings of aircraft is intense because once your engines are on the wings you get a 30-year stream of spare parts and there is virtually no competition for the parts for your engine. As a manufacturer of jet engines you are therefore willing to buy the airplane for the airline and lease it to them and give them an operating lease that is cancellable pre-delivery and up to one year post-delivery. If their business turns down they just give the plane back and you get to keep it.

We figured out the value for wide-bodied and narrow-bodied aircraft (Figure 3.33). For narrow-bodied aircraft like 727s the cancellation feature was worth 83% of the value of the engines. The company CEO was afraid to stop offering the cancellation feature for fear of losing all the customers. We then performed a market segmentation based on the volatility of passenger revenue miles, airline by airline, in order to determine when the option should be exercised. This is when the value of operating the plane falls, which falls when passenger revenue miles fall. Airlines that have no variability in passenger revenue miles would never return the plane if they do their analysis correctly. The ones with enormous volatility will have a much higher probability of returning the plane and for them the options will be more valuable. Generally speaking, the higher the variance of the underlining risky asset the more valuable the option is. The company therefore stopped offering the cancellation feature to the

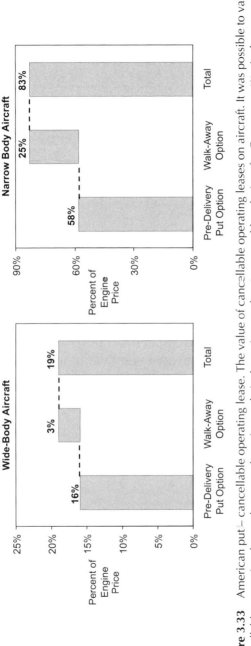

Figure 3.33 American put – cancellable operating lease. The value of cancellable operating leases on aircraft. It was possible to value cancellable operating leases because there is a relatively active market in second-hand aircraft. *Comments:* (1) single source of uncertainty – price of second-hand aircraft; (2) option value significantly underestimated by management; (3) leasing strategy changed.

10% of their customers that had the highest volatility in passenger revenue miles. In 1991 and 1992, there was a mild recession and passenger revenue miles decreased and the airlines that were doing the worst started returning the planes to the manufacturers, but not to our client, who calculated that it saved US$200 million by means of this analysis.

4.4. Consumer PC assembly business: exit decision

The following example concerns switching options. Figure 3.34 shows some work that was done around 1996 for an assembler of consumer PCs. The factories in this business are very expensive to operate. The rate of growth in sales is double digit and on the right-hand side you see that the EVA® was negative for all the companies illustrated here except for Gateway, which was the only one earning more than its cost of capital.

The computer memory (DRAM) business continually experiences major fluctuations in prices. The question for most operators is how long to stay in the business haemorrhaging cash before it turns around and becomes a great business again. The answer is to look at the problem as a switching option. A switching option is where you have the right to turn something off and then turn it on again at a later date. In the case of personal computer assembly, if the cost of exiting was zero and the cost of re-entering was zero people would turn off their factories right away and wait until circumstances changed and then turn them back on again. It turns out that the cost of re-entering the business is about one half year's revenues and when you work this out as a switching option and compare it with net present value and EVA® you get very different answers.

When the gross margin of the company is 13% (Figure 3.35), all indicators say stay open, except for economic profit, which is actually negative because return on invested capital is 7.6% and the weighted average cost of capital is 13.7%. You can see that as the margin falls to 11% even net present value is negative, but real options say that if you are currently in operation you should stay in operation because of the cost of getting out of that operation and re-entering it. On the other hand, if you are not in operation real options tell you not to enter the market.

Some actual numbers are shown in Figure 3.36. By the way, our client had a gross operating margin that was off the scale on the down side so the actual answer was to exit immediately even using real options. In fact, they did not exit then, but two years later after losing an additional US$1.2 billion. I mention this because I want to point out that real options do not justify everything. The cost of doing things is often higher than the value of the option. If you take a look at the 11% line you can see that EVA® is negative, net present value is negative, but because of the cost of switch-

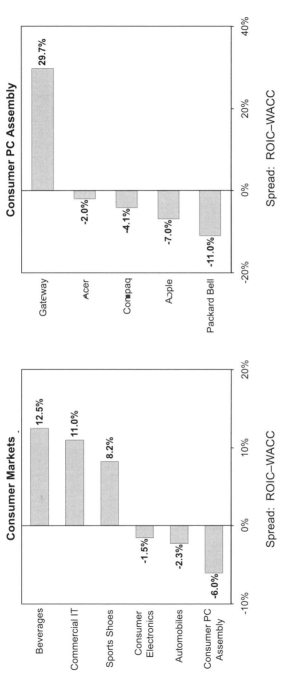

Figure 3.34 Switching option: exit and re-entry decision. Despite the strong growth, consumer PC assembly players have found their market participation to be mostly dissatisfying as they are not earning their cost of capital (*source*: Analyst Reports; Annual Statements).

Valuation Methodologies

Scenario	ROA	NPV	Economic Profit (WACC = 13.7%)
In Operation, Gross Margin = 13%	Continue	Continue	Exit (ROIC = 7.6%)
In Operation, Gross Margin = 11%	Continue	Exit	Exit (ROIC = 5.6%)
Not in Operation	Don't Enter	Don't Enter	Don't Enter (ROIC = 7.6%)

Figure 3.35   ROA (Return on Assets) gives different decisions than NPV and economic profit. Traditional valuation techniques give mixed decisions about whether the unprofitable players should immediately exist the business. However, ROA suggests that players should stay in the market and exit only if conditions do not improve.

Valuation Methodologies

Gross Operating Margin	ROA* NPV + Flexibility Value	NPV Σ (Cash Flows)	Economic Profit (Short Term) (ROIC–WACC) x IC
15%	$2.98	$2.62	$0.05
13%	$1.71	$1.02	-$0.07**
11%	$0.79	-$0.59	-$0.09
9%	$0.36	-$1.79	-$0.11

Figure 3.36   ROA gives different values of staying in business than NPV and EP. ROA gives significantly different value to the business than EP and NPV approaches (1997, USD billions). *Assume a volatility of 16% annually for the gross operating margin (GOM). **ROIC before taxes = 7.6%, tax rate = 30%, WACC = 13.7%, invested capital is 26% of sales of $3.6 billion.

ing it pays to stay in the business. In fact, the difference between the real options answer and the net present value answer was about US$1.4 billion. $0.79 - (-0.59) = 1.38$

4.5. Plant construction: multiphase investment

In Figure 3.37 you can see work done around 1997 for a commodity chemical producer. Commodity chemicals are hugely cyclical businesses. When the profits widen everyone starts to build new factories and the profits narrow and people stop building factories and so the process continues. The traditional net present value analysis was conducted by looking at when the expenditures would be incurred to build the plant. There was US$50 million for a design phase in the first six months, US$200 million for a pre-construction phase in the next six months and then US$400 million for final construction and then revenues started. That was the timing of expected cash flows, which were discounted producing a number of US$70 million or US$80 million negative. What you see here is a compound option; any phased investment is a compound option where you have to complete the first phase to do the second phase. However, you don't have to do the second phase, you can stop. You have to complete the second phase to do the third phase but you don't have to do the third phase, you can stop. So when they looked at this as a compound option they realised that they had a decision point today about whether or not to start or not start, but if they started they only committed themselves to US$50 million of design. They had another decision point at the end of six months and if the spread widened they would continue; if the spread had narrowed they would not continue. As it turned out, the spread had widened so they continued into the pre-construction work and at the end of that phase the spread had widened still further so they completed their chemical plant about six months earlier than their nearest competitor and they got the full spread on the new volume for six months when nobody else was coming into the market.

4.6. Natural resources: exploration and development

A compound rainbow option (Figure 3.38) is shown in the following example, which concerns the exploration and production of a major integrated oil company. The decision about when to develop a field is an important decision in the life of every company because the investments are so enormous. The field is first explored using sonics and then drilling is started. The question is at what point you stop drilling and start developing, because developing brings the cash flows in to the present. A huge debate starts within the company somewhere around the 50% point. Some people say that the cash flow should be brought into the present by

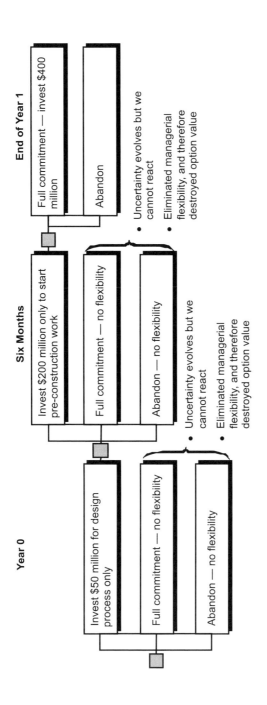

Figure 3.37 Compound option – multiphase investment. The value of compound options in plant construction. Today (year 0), management does not need to commit to the entire project; it can simply begin the design process (at a cost of US$50 million) and learn more about the operating spread uncertainty. Six months later, management has a similar option, to begin the pre-construction process without a full commitment and learn more about the uncertainties. At the end of the year, management no longer has the flexibility to learn more about the uncertainty and must choose between a full commitment or abandonment.

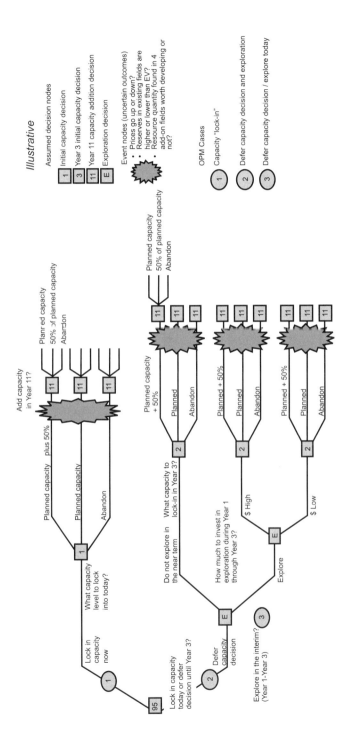

Figure 3.38 Compound rainbow option for exploration and development. The decision tree shows a stylised version of the decision to develop a large energy resource. There were two sources of uncertainty; the price of energy and the amount of resource in the ground, and there were compound options.

developing now with 50% of the field unexplored and other people say if you do that you are bound to wrong-size the investment because you will be investing on the basis of the expectation that there is oil in the ground, which is uncertain as there is a lot of variability in sonics.

If you build the billion-dollar refinery and there is more oil in the ground than you thought, you have to build half a refinery and that is very inefficient. If there is less oil in the ground than you thought, you have invested too much and you have wasted capital. Usually somewhere between the 50% and 100% point a decision is made to develop the field. The threshold in this case was around the 60%: 60% had been explored by drilling, 40% by sonics. The debate was raging within management and it was suggested that we should look at this as an option problem because it is a multiphased investment. We can choose to lock in capacity today by investing today or we can defer that investment and if we defer the investment we can decide to explore or not to explore. If we decide to explore we can do it at a high level, a medium level or a low level. Once the information is in from exploration three years from now (this is decision point two but Year 3) we can decide how much capacity to add. There is another decision point in Year 11 based on long-term growth in demand. The company therefore looked at this as an option problem, a multiphased compound option problem and a rainbow option problem, because there is more than one source of uncertainty: there is uncertainty about the price of a barrel of oil and there is uncertainty about the quantity of oil in the ground. You can solve this type of problem on an Excel spreadsheet, although at the time we used more powerful means. The answer was that the base case, which was no exploration and immediate development, would have a value of 100 and the option value was 225 where they decided to explore first at a high level and then make a decision in Year 3.

The first companies to use real options were the integrated oil companies Royal Dutch Shell, Texaco, Exxon, British Petroleum, Mobil and Amoco. It made a lot of sense to them. Engineers were not unaccustomed to using technical analysis for looking at things like this and it became a very natural fit. Other companies that are using this are power-generating companies. Enron, for example, used switching options for pricing peak load capacity. PC assemblers are using switching options, the transportation industry is using switching options and the pharmaceutical industry is beginning to use switching options.

4.7. Capital expenditures: a programme

Let me finish off with a discussion of the examples. When you think about your capital expenditures I'm sure that you think about them one at

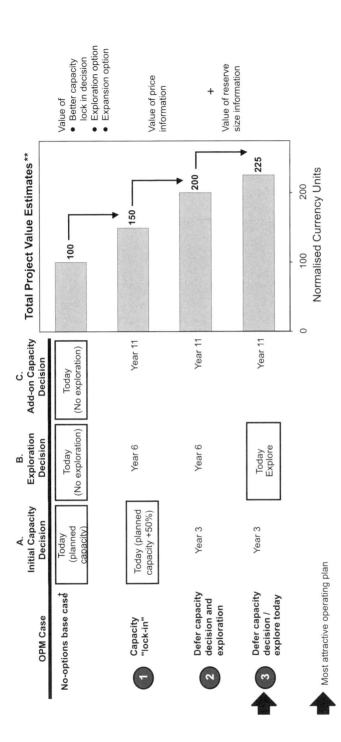

Figure 3.39 ROA model valuation results*. The optimal solution provided more than twice the value and was completely different from the client's base case. * Throughout the document the results have been normalised and rounded off to provide general insights while maintaining client confidentiality. ** For comparison purposes and because of lack of information, each of the 4 cases assume a Year 1 exploration cost equal to 0; if 'best-guess' exploration. † Analogous to traditional DCF case (i.e., assumes deterministic inputs and no managerial flexibility).

a time. You look at the new factory or the new product development programme, you look at the R&D programme for a given drug. Option pricing says that you should be looking at them as an entire programme over a period of time instead of looking at them as one investment at a time. I'll give you a simple example to show you the difference. One of our clients was going to spend about a billion dollars on capital spending over the next five years and basically could build two big plants or four medium-sized plants. The big plants had lower costs per unit, the medium-sized plants were more expensive and they had a lower net present value. However, if you look at it as a capital expenditure pro-gramme, you begin to realise that there are some advantages to building medium-sized plants. If you had four medium-sized plants you could locate them in different geographies and you can move production among the plants to respond to local demand and therefore cut distribu-tion costs. If there is a breakdown and you have two big plants you lose half of your capacity during the breakdown; if there is a breakdown in a medium-sized plant you loose only a quarter of your capacity. When the big plants are completed they have excess capacity that extends for a period of time, while the medium-sized plants have less excess capacity when they are completed. Therefore, it is not clear that the advantage of lower cost per unit of the big plants is more valuable than the flexibility of the higher cost per unit medium-sized plants. You can use option pricing to measure the flexibility in the system.

Corporate finance should include thinking about the entire capital expenditure system. This obviously extends to mergers and acquisitions as well. Most companies look at acquisitions one at a time, but they should be looking at acquisitions as a programme. When you complete the first acquisition what does it lead to? Does it give you any options for other acquisitions that follow it? If it does, your mergers and acquisitions pro-gramme is a cohesive flexible programme, which is more valuable than a one-off acquisition. So the first acquisition on its own might have a nega-tive net present value, but as part of a programme it might have a positive value.

4.8. Project analysis: a four-step process

There is a four-step process for dealing with such matters (Figure 3.40). The first step is to calculate the net present value of the project. But when you calculate the present value of the project you are calculating the project using expected cash flows and you are implicitly assuming no flexibility so that becomes the base case to which real options must reduce when you take away the flexibility.

The second step is to model the entire process as a decision tree. This gives the project a certain value today with its expected cash flows and the value can go up or down tomorrow. The amount by which it goes up or down is the uncertainty that is modelled using Monte Carlo techniques. The greater the uncertainty the more it goes up and goes down in one time period, so there is a defined relationship between the estimated uncertainty in the distribution of returns that comes out of a Monte Carlo analysis and the up and down movements in a decision tree. The third step is to put decisions into the tree: decisions to expand, contract, abandon, extend and defer with the computer choosing the maximum of each of those activities at each node in the tree. The final step is to price the tree correctly using real options analysis which basically involves finding the value of a project by creating a portfolio that has the same payouts as the option on the project. If you know the value of the portfolio you know the value of the option. This last part is a little tricky. For the technical details I would like to refer you to my latest book on 'real options'. Needless to say, the material is being worked over by many different people now and it is actually becoming practicable and useable. Real options are increasingly being used in the field of valuation and a lot of work is being done at the cutting edge. I have applied real options six times to value internet companies during the past few years. Because of their scale, internet companies can be treated like a project and the optionality becomes important (Figure 3.41).

NOTE BY THE EDITORS

Real options promise to bridge the gap between scenarios and strategies and capture the value of managerial flexibility to adapt decisions in response to unexpected market developments. Companies create shareholder value by identifying, managing and exercising real options associated with their investment portfolio. The real options method applies financial options theory to quantify the value of management flexibility in a world of uncertainty. If used as a conceptual tool, the method allows management to characterise and communicate the strategic value of an investment project. Strategies that do not provide guidance for action are of no use, but on the other hand, strategies that are implemented without considering the changing business environment, are also dangerous. A strategy in that case means that opportunities are missed, or that actions are stuck to even though they do not optimise value creation. Flexibility must therefore be incorporated into strategic plans. Option thinking can provide this flexibility. Traditional methods, such as net present value, fail to accurately capture the economic value of

Step One

- Complete the base case present value (without flexibility) based on
  - Expected future cash flows
  - Cost of capital based on comparables

Note that the expected value of the project evolves through time as shown in the figure to the right

Step Two

- Estimate the volatility of the value of the project in order to derive the volatility of the rate of return
  - A Monte Carlo approach can combine many uncertainties
  - The volatility of the drivers of uncertainty may be estimated from internal data or from subjective estimates made by management

The output is a binomial lattice in value

$$u = e^{\sigma\sqrt{T}}, \quad d = 1/u$$

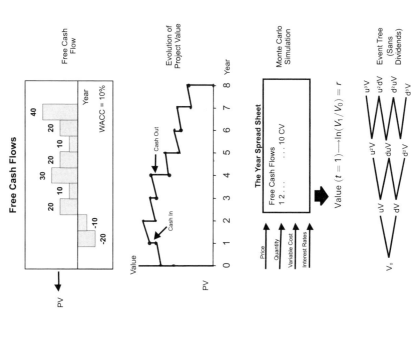

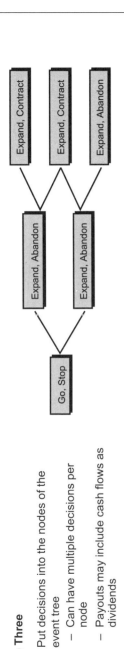

Step Three

- Put decisions into the nodes of the event tree
  - Can have multiple decisions per node
  - Payouts may include cash flows as dividends

Step Four

- Work backward in the tree (unless there is path dependency) to obtain values at each node and to make optimal decisions
  - Use no arbitrage condition to conform to law of "one price"
  - Output is the value of the project with flexibility and decision rules

Figure 3.40 Project analysis: a four-step process

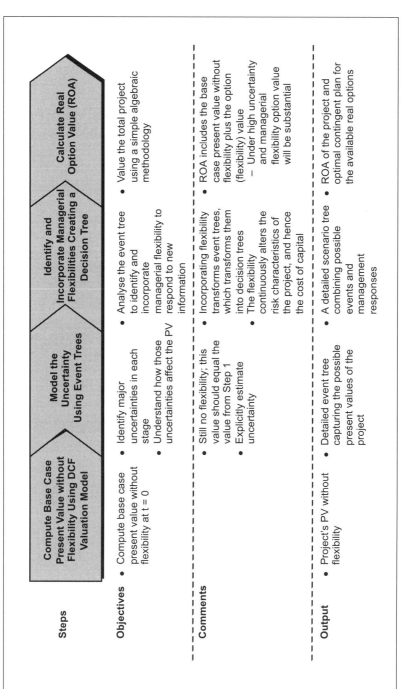

Figure 3.41 Project analysis. Overall approach – a four-step process.

investments in an environment of widespread uncertainty and rapid change. The real options method is a new state-of-the-art technique for the valuation and management of strategic investments. It enables corporate decision-makers to leverage upon uncertainty and limit downside risk.

Chapter 4

Value-based management

Control processes to create value through integration

Geert Scheipers

Geert Scheipers holds a Master's degree in Commercial & Financial Sciences, and is a specialist in banking and finance. He was awarded the degree of Master in Controllership at the Vlerick Leuven Gent Management School (VLGMS). Scheipers has considerable practical experience in the field of management accounting and control, serving presently as senior consultant at B&M Consulting. He is specifically interested in linking the latest academic developments with practitioners' insights in the domain of strategy development and implementation, value-based management, ABC/M and the balanced scorecard. In addition, he is guest lecturer at the VLGMS, is member of the editorial staff of the Belgian Institute of Management Accountants and Controllers and is author of a number of articles and papers within the field of 'Strategy' and 'Control'.

Anne Ameels

Anne Ameels is management accounting and control research assistant at the Vlerick Leuven Gent Management School. Her research focuses on value-based management, balanced scorecard and activity-based costing and activity-based management. She is author of a number of articles and papers within those research fields. Ameels studied Applied Economics (Ghent University) and holds an MBA degree in Financial Management (Vlerick Leuven Gent Management School).

Werner Bruggeman

Werner Bruggeman is Professor in Management Accounting and Control at the Ghent University and at the Vlerick Leuven Gent Management School. He is Partner at the Vlerick Leuven Gent Management School and Managing Partner at B&M Consulting, specialising in implementing integrated performance measurement and activity-based cost management systems. His research concentrates on the relationship between strategy, organisation and management control. Bruggeman is highly experienced in consultancy, especially in the design and implementation of costing and performance measurement systems.

1. INTRODUCTION

During the past few decades, management accounting has faced increasing challenges to adopt new approaches, designed to fit the changes in the economic environment and to correct perceived inefficiencies in existing controlling structures.

In the 1950s and 1960s, an important debate focused on the character of information for decision-making. Another group of scholars addressed the issue of whether the contribution margin approach was superior to systems that fully allocated overheads. In the 1970s, several researchers flocked around the topic of residual income and the optimal control of relatively autonomous divisions.

More recently, with new developments in management accounting it appears that three letter acronyms are becoming very popular. Some of the most fashionable are: SMA (strategic management accounting); ABC, ABM & ABB (activity-based costing and its variants activity-based management and activity-based budgeting); BPR (business process re-engineering); and BSC (balanced scorecard). A common element, which distinguishes the later management accounting tools from the earlier ones, is that the more recent *apparati* have emerged predominantly from practice and from consultants. Another modern-day 'hot' topic in practice, which is claimed to be changing financial management at the highest level in some of the world's largest companies (Bromwich, 1998) is value-based management (VBM).

This chapter presents the results of a literature review of the approaches that these practitioners and consultants have developed concerning the pursuit of shareholder value. The objective is to assess the potential of these approaches in order to ensure that the resources of organisations are obtained and used effectively and efficiently in the accomplishment of their objectives. The rationale for this chapter is the perceived gap in the literature with regard to an overview of the value-based management practices offered.

The first section of the chapter is a brief description of VBM. Here we describe the history behind VBM, propose a general definition and give some insights to its application. The second section pursues the matter of performance measurement and the third introduces the most common valuation tools that are being used in VBM systems. Because metrics are not the end to a VBM programme, in the fourth section we describe the kind of ingredients that are indispensable in a well-designed VBM system; the methodology we use is a review of the literature concerning the integrated approach of six high-profile management consulting firms. The fifth and last section provides some conclusions.

2. VALUE-BASED MANAGEMENT

2.1. Value-based management in perspective

Value-based management is a management control system that measures, encourages and supports the creation of net worth. From the mainstream management accounting viewpoint, the concept of control systems results from the suboptimal behavioural consequences of the "agency" theory. From the perspective of a firm regarded as a set of contracts among factors of production with each factor motivated by its self-interest, a separation of the control of the firm on the one hand and the ownership of the firm, on the other hand, is an efficient form of economic organisation (Fama, 1980). However, this separation can simultaneously cause austere dysfunctional behaviour.

The agency theory focuses on the agency relationship between the actor or the group (the agent), which has certain obligations to fulfil for another actor or group (the principal) because of their economic relationship. The selection of appropriate governance mechanisms between the agent and the principal is (given the assumption that agents are motivated by their self-interest) necessary to ensure an efficient alignment of their interests. This alignment in interests can be disrupted by two main problems: the agency problem and the problem of risk sharing.

The agency problem is based on the assumption that the desires and goals of the agents and principals can conflict; and that it is difficult or expensive for the principal to monitor what the agent is doing (Eisenhardt, 1989). The problem of risk sharing is based on the assumption that the principal and the agent have different attitudes towards risks, which explains their different courses of action (Shankman, 1999).

Both problems are the corollary of a lack of goal congruence between the objectives of the agents and those of the principals of the organisation. The central purpose of management control systems is to lead people to take actions in accordance with their perceived self-interest that are also in the best interest of the organisation (Anthony and Govindarajan, 2001). Value-based management systems are conceived to reduce this lack of goal congruence. Moreover, the various proponents of VBM systems think they have a very good answer to both problems outlined in the agency theory by trying to make managers think and behave more like owners.

2.2. Defining value-based management (VBM)

Although there is an ongoing polemic regarding the metrics that should be used and initially even more who could claim the copyright on them, we see that apart from which management approach or process is used, VBM measures are generally based on comparison between (a) corporate market value and corporate accounting book value and/or (b) on the residual income measure (Bromwich, 1998). Moreover, it seems that even in the way the different practices are being described, authors tend to veil their concepts in mist. We find, however, that most definitions of value-based management are a sign of the same way of thinking.

A first set of publicists describes the output of value-based management:

- Value-based management is essentially a management approach whereby companies' driving philosophy is to maximise shareholder value by producing returns in excess of the cost of capital (Simms, 2001).
- Value-based management is a framework for measuring and, more importantly, managing businesses to create superior long-term value for shareholders that satisfies both the capital and product markets (Ronte, 1998).
- Value-based management is a framework for measuring and managing businesses to create superior long-term value for shareholders. Rewards are measured in terms of enhanced share price performance and dividend growth (Marsh, 1999).
- Value-based management is a management philosophy that uses analytical tools and processes to focus an organisation on the single objective of creating shareholder value (Condon and Goldstein, 1998).
- Value-based management is a new way for managing, focused on the creation of real value not paper profits. Real value is created when a company makes returns that fully compensate investors for the total costs involved in the investment, plus a premium that more than compensates for the additional risk incurred (Christopher and Ryals, 1999).
- Value-based management is based on the notion that the central objectives for all public traded companies are to maximise shareholder value. Because it offers companies a logical and systematic way to pursue improvements in shareholder value, it has received considerable action in the business press (Bannister and Jesuthasan, 1997).
- Value-based management is a term that describes a management philosophy based on managing a firm with economic value creation principles (Armitage and Fog, 1996).

A second group focuses on the combination of the process and the outcome:

- Value-based management is a combination of beliefs, principles and processes that effectively arm the company to succeed in the battle against competition from the outside and the institutional imperative from the inside.

These beliefs, principles and processes form the basis of a systematic approach to achieving the company's governing objective (McTaggart *et al.*, 1994).

- Value-based management [...] can be all embracing. It aligns strategies, policies, performance, measures, rewards, organisation, processes, people, and systems to deliver increased shareholder value (Black *et al.*, 1998).
- Value-based management is a managerial approach in which the primary purpose is shareholder wealth maximisation with the objective of the firm, its systems, strategy, processes, analytical techniques, performance measurements and culture as their guiding objective shareholder wealth maximisation (Arnold, 1998).
- Value-based management is a management approach which puts shareholder value creation at the centre of the company philosophy. The maximisation of shareholder value directs company strategy, structure and processes, it governs executive remuneration and dictates what measures are used to monitor performance (KPMG Consulting, 1999).
- The founding principle underlying value-based management is the discounted cash model of firm value. However, VBM is more than a performance measurement system. Proponents argue that if it is to be successful it must be used to tie performance to compensation. The guiding principle underlying the use of VBM, then, is that measuring and rewarding activities that create shareholder value will ultimately lead to greater shareholder value (Martin and Petty, 2000).
- Value-based management says, in a nutshell, the key to increased shareholder value lies in the integration of strategic planning, performance measurement and compensation (Leahy, 2000).
- Value-based management is a different way of focusing an organisation's strategic and financial management processes. In order to maximise value, the whole organisation must be involved (Anonymous, 1998).

We found only one source that describes just the process:

- Value-based management is a holistic management approach that encompasses redefined goals, redesigned structures and systems, rejuvenated strategic and operational processes, and revamped human resources practices. Value-based management is not a quick fix but a path requiring persistence and commitment (Boulos *et al.*, 2001).

The references that define inputs, process and outputs of value-based management are scarce:

- An approach to management whereby the company's overall aspirations, analytical techniques and management processes are aligned to help the company maximise its value by focusing management decision-making on the key drivers of shareholder value (Institute of Management Accountants, 1997).

In general, the distinctive features of value-based management are:

- *Management* – VBM is a management tool, a control system; an apparatus that is used to integrate resources and tasks towards the achievement of stated organisational goals (Merchant, 1998).
- *Approach* – VBM is a prescribed and usually repetitious way of carrying out an activity or a set of activities that propagate its values all over the organisation. It is a robust disciplined process that is meant to be apparent in the heart of all business decisions (Morin and Jarrell, 2001).
- *Maximising shareholder value* – VBM's purpose is to generate as much net worth as possible. Or put in another way: to distribute the given resources to the most valuable investments. Maximisation also implies a forward vision, based on expected outcomes.

2.3. Why value-based management?

As in every economic trade-off, managers are confronted with optimising the allocation of scarce resources. The current economic and social environment, characterised by countless changes and evolutions (Young and O'Byrne, 2001), provides management and more particularly those in management accounting and management control positions, with new challenges. Those challenges not only reveal inefficiencies in the existing management systems, but also support the need for an integrated management tool. The most important challenges and inefficiencies are briefly discussed below.

In the Anglo-Saxon countries and more recently also in continental Europe much attention is directed towards the issue of shareholder value (Mills and Weinstein, 2000; Young and O'Byrne, 2001). The attention for shareholder value has always been on the management agenda, but in the 1960s and the 1990s the focus on shareholder value was less explicit. A McKinsey & Co study reveals that shareholder-oriented economies appear to perform better than other economic systems, and other stakeholders do not suffer at the hands of shareholders (Copeland *et al.*, 2000).

Furthermore, it appears that there is a paradigm shift with regard to management objectives. In the past (and probably still even these days in some organisations) sales growth or revenue growth was often the governing objective. Residual income theory applied to customer or product profitability analysis reveals that not every type of growth is a good thing to pursue.

This is however not the only change in management objectives, since management increasingly realises that traditional earning measures do not reflect real value creation. Those traditional metrics are accounting-based and therefore do not take into account the risk notion, nor do they consider the impacts of inflation, or opportunity costs. Stern Stewart, (1999) calls this: 'The switch from "managing for earning" to "managing for value".'

In addition, value is said to be one of the best performance measures because it is the only measure that requires complete information. To understand value creation one must use a long-term strategic point of view, manage all cash flows on the income statement and movements on the balance sheet, and must know how to compare cash flows from different time periods on a risk adjusted basis. It is therefore impossible to make good decisions without complete information and, according to Copeland et al. (2000), there is no performance metric other than value that uses complete information.

Companies are looking for an approach that serves as many purposes as possible. The VBM approaches are argued to subsume or render un-necessary most, if not all, other types of performance measures at the corporate and strategic business unit levels. They therefore contest the principle of different accounting for different purposes. Bromwich (1998), but also Ottosen and Weissenrieder (1996), mention the search for com-prehensive systems. Bromwich observes the need for measuring tools, applicable to different organisational levels, such as the corporate and business unit level, while Ottosen and Weissenrieder emphasise the need for measurement systems that can be used for internal and external communication.

In recent times, business executives have concentrated on improving 'operational' processes such as manufacturing, supply chain, sales and marketing, etc. All too often, these activities have resulted in improve-ments that do not deserve the predicate 'sustainable'. Kotter (1995) notes that the vast majority of major change processes have failed to produce the results expected for the reason that they miss an important ingredient. This ingredient is a lack of corresponding changes in the business management processes and in the organisational culture. A lack of changes regarding an economic focus or unclarity about how capital is to be deployed and managed in the future, among other things, serves to underline the sustainability of these operational changes.

2.4. The stakeholder approach versus the shareholder approach

Managers in all kinds of organisations are now faced with the dilemma of how to reconcile the competing claims of shareholders and other stake-holders. Top management's concern with shareholder value has never been greater, as mentioned above. But, on the other hand, the interest in stakeholder approaches to strategic management is also growing around the world (Mills and Weinstein, 2000; Young and O'Byrne, 2001).

Business is all about creating value. This value creation process is only possible with the support of different stakeholder groups. Despite the fact that the objectives of different stakeholder groups do not always converge, they do realise that working together to realise the multiple goals of the firm is the only way to reach some of their own objectives.

At first sight, the literature suggests a major distinction between the stakeholder and the shareholder approach. However, when we look at the interpretation and observations of Grant (1998) according to the shareholder theory, we detect a close similarity between his viewpoint and that of Mills and Weinstein. Indeed, Mills and Weinstein (2000) point out that the shareholder and the stakeholder principle do not have to conflict if the issues of the measurement of value and the distribution of value are looked at separately. They state the belief that the quest to create value is important for all organisations. The efficient use of resources should involve ensuring that an economic return in excess of the cost of capital is achieved. However, the wealth created does not have to be distributed with the primacy of the shareholder in mind. There is no reason why other stakeholders with legitimate claims should not be a key part of the distribution process.

'Socially responsible business behaviour', as defined by Rappaport (1998), integrates the statements of Pruzan (1998) – who believes that most traditional business thinking is based and dominated by the concept of shareholder accountability – with the conclusions of Mills and Weinstein. This behaviour is described as an alternative stakeholder approach, consistent with shareholder interests without neglecting other stakeholder groups and the emphasis on the competitiveness of the organisation.

Value-based management, as an approach to encourage management in the value creation process and more particularly in the maximisation of shareholder value, does not have to conflict with the stakeholder approach if the value-based management process within the organisation is combined with 'socially responsible business behaviour'.

3. VALUE-BASED PERFORMANCE METRICS

3.1. Introduction

In management accounting literature it is often said that one can tell whether a subject is in fashion when lots of different measures, all claiming to be the paramount performance indicator, are competing against each other. Another symptom of a so-called 'hype' could be the fact that numerous acronyms are proposed to describe an identical framework (Armitage and Fog, 1996). Both consultants and academics strive for an extensive platform and describe numerous value-based performance measures like EVA®, EP, CFROI or SVA.

In most cases, the development of these measures is based on widespread criticism of commonly used profit-related measures, such as return on investment, return on assets, earnings before interest, taxes and amortisation of goodwill or earnings per share (Günther, 1997; Mills *et al.*, 1998). Some of the value-based measures have been developed recently; others have existed for decennia or have been derived from the capital market theory to be used for divisional controlling. We found references on value-based measures in both practitioner-oriented publications and academic journals, but also noticed that more and more mainstream corporate finance and investment textbooks are covering these new performance metrics.

In this chapter we discuss a non-exhaustive number of value-based metrics. The value of an organisation can be gauged from two different angles. Value-enhancing managers are considered to be those who create value by increasing the company's value relative to the cost of capital at their disposal. Managers whose accounting investments exceed the market value of their business are said to be destroying value. From the first point of view, the stock market data provide us with the information needed to calculate the value of the company unambiguously. We will call this approach the *listed perspective*. On the other hand, many companies (and obviously all unlisted organisations) estimate the warranted value of their common stock indirectly, using an alternative valuation model. In this way, these performance measures can very well be used to assess divisional performance and to provide information supporting decisions at the corporate or divisional level. Here, we will call this method of quantifying value, the *not-listed perspective*.

3.2. Listed perspective

Total shareholder return

A first approach to measure shareholder value from the perspective of a quoted company is total shareholder return (TSR); that is, share price appreciation plus dividends.

$$\text{Total Shareholder Return} = \frac{(P_{t+1} - P_t) + D_{t+1}}{P_t}$$

where P = Share price and D = Dividends paid.

In a recent INSEAD survey, Boulos *et al.* (2001) state that TSR is applied in 7.4% of the companies that used value-based measures. TSR represents the change in capital value of a company over a one-year period, plus dividends, expressed as a plus or minus percentage of the opening value. Rappaport (1987) considers a company's stock price as the clearest measure of market expectations of its performance. The capital markets are distinctively focused on the overall rate of return of any stock, which in addition to the stream of dividend appreciation also includes capital appreciation but excludes share repurchase.

Total shareholder return is also documented as shareholder rate of return or as total business return. The latter idiom is typically used by Boston Consulting Group. Although TSR is an unbiased measure of the return for the shareholder (Morin and Jarrell, 2001), it provides a direct link to external measurement because it must be reported under US GAAP in SEC filings (Smith, 1997) and it anticipates the future value and the expected risk (Rappaport, 1986). There are, however, a few shortcomings in the use of TSR. Firstly, as it can only be calculated for companies that are listed on the stock exchange, it cannot be used to calculate shareholder return at business unit level or for specific product/market combinations. Secondly, some authors claim that TSR is not an efficient indicator to judge managers' performance because it is driven by many factors beyond the control of the firm's executives (Bacidore *et al.*, 1997; Bannister and Jesuthasan, 1997).

Market value added

The difference between the equity market valuation of a company and the sum of the adjusted book value of debt and equity invested in the company is called market value added (MVA). According to the INSEAD survey mentioned above, 7.9% of respondents claim to use MVA as a proxy for shareholder value.

$$MVA = \text{Market value} - \text{Invested capital}$$

Market value added is said to be unique in its ability to gauge shareholder value creation because it captures both valuation – the degree of wealth enrichment for the shareholders and performance; that is, the market assessment of how effectively a firm's managers have used the scarce resources under their control – as well as how effectively management has positioned the company in the long term (Ehrbar, 1998). Furthermore, MVA avoids subjective accounting issues regarding anticipation of future cash flows and discount rates because it approximates the stock market estimation of net present value (Hillman and Keim, 2001). Although we noted that little research has been conducted on the predicting power of MVA, it is said to be a more effective investment tool than other measures.[1] In a recent study, Yook and McCabe (2001) examined the cross-section of expected stock returns between 1985 and 1994 and found evidence of a strong negative relationship between MVA and average stock returns.

3.3. Not-listed perspective

When unambiguous stock market data are not available, the proxy for value creation should be calculated on the basis of information from within the company. This often implies reliance on financial statements. The conventional structure of financial statements creates some obstacles to an articulation between a (multi-period) measure of excess value created and a matching (multi-period) assessment of accounting flows. The shortcomings of accounting-based measurements are numerous: alternative accounting measures may be employed, risk is excluded, investment requirements are excluded, dividend policy is not considered, the time value of money is ignored (Rappaport, 1986), errors occur at different stages of project life, errors occur when firms or divisions have a balanced mix of old and new projects (Brealey and Myers, 2000) and poor correlation of profit-related performance measures with the valuation used on capital markets (Günther, 1997). To overcome these shortcomings, adjustments can be made to the underlying figures or to the metric itself in order to reflect value added more accurately.

Various authors (Bromwich and Walker, 1998; Ittner and Larcker, 1998; Dechow *et al.*, 1999; O'Hanlon and Peasnell, 2001) have stated that residual income can be considered the basis for many value-based metrics. Residual income is defined as the accounting income attributable to shareholders at the end of the period minus the accounting book value of shareholders' funds at the end of the previous period multiplied by the cost of capital. It provides a clear indication of whether a firm has made enough profit to satisfy both creditors and equity holders (Eiteman *et al.*, 1999). Besides the residual income-based measures that evaluate the generated shareholder value ex-post for a single period, one can also gauge the value of a company by discounting future cash flows or free cash flows based on forecasts for a multi-period planning horizon. We will therefore subdivide this perspective in single period measures and multi-period metrics.

---

[1]More specifically: market value of equity, book/price value ratio and price/earnings ratio.

Single period metrics

Economic value added

Economic value added (EVA®) is the most straightforward antecedent of residual income. It is also considered to be the best known of the shareholder value metrics (Brown *et al.*, 2000). More than 47% of the respondents in the INSEAD survey claim to use EVA as the economic profit measure (Haspeslagh *et al.*, 2001).

$$EVA® = NOPAT - (K_c * Capital)$$

or

$$\underset{\text{debt + equity}}{}$$

$$EVA® = (r - K_c) * Capital$$

where NOPAT[2] = Income available to common equity + Increase in equity equivalents[3] + Interest expenses after taxes + Preferred dividends + Minority interest provisions OR Sales – Operating expenses (including Depreciation) – Taxes. Capital = Common equity + Equity equivalents + Debt + Preferred stock + Minority interest OR Adjusted current assets – Non-interest-bearing current liabilities + Net fixed assets. K_c = Cost of capital. r = Rate of return on capital.

EVA® and related measures attempt to improve on traditional accounting measures of performance by measuring the economic profit of an enterprise. Economic value added is defined as net operating profit after tax (NOPAT) less a company's cost of capital (including the cost of both equity and debt) (Morin and Jarrell, 2001). NOPAT equals the sum of income available to common equity plus the increase in equity equivalents plus interest expenses after taxes plus preferred dividends plus minority interest provisions.

When NOPAT is divided by adjusted book value of capital, we abandon the residual income formula and note that EVA® can also be computed by taking the spread between the rate of return on capital and the cost of capital, multiplied by the economic book value of the capital committed to the business (O'Hanlon and Peasnell, 1998).

When EVA® is projected and discounted to a present value it accounts for the market value that management adds to, or subtracts from, the capital it has employed (G. B. Stewart, 1999). This relationship between MVA and EVA® is the theoretical foundation for Stern Stewart's management system. In line with residual income theory, business success is

---

[2] NOPAT differs from NOPLAT (used in earlier chapters) in so far as it excludes tax deferrals.

[3] Equity equivalents gross up the standard accounting into what G. B. Stewart (1999) calls 'economic book value'. They eliminate accounting distortions by converting from accrual to cash accounting.

defined in terms of the present value of future EVA® measures. G. B. Stewart's claim that EVA® is the only performance measure that ties directly to the intrinsic market value of any company (Dodd and Chen, 1996) is also true when taking into consideration all metrics that are being used in the residual income-based valuation framework; these include economic profit, shareholder value added, economic value creation but also shareholder value analysis.

Both academics and practitioners point out the numerous benefits of EVA®. Because it is a single-period measure, it allows for an annual measurement of actual not-estimated or forecasted value created performance (Armitage and Fog, 1996). Others refer to the fact that it corresponds more closely to economic profit than accounting earnings do and, as an objective, is consistent with the pursuit of shareholder interest (Grant, 1998; Young and O'Byrne, 2001). Claims have also been made that EVA® can drive behavioural change by providing the incentive for managers to promote shareholder wealth as the primary objective (Dodd and Chen, 1996; Biddle *et al.*, 1997; Brewer *et al.*, 1999; McLaren, 1999).

Although some research indicates that EVA® indeed is quite well correlated with stock price performance (O'Byrne, 1996; Lehn and Makhija, 1996; Bacidore *et al.*, 1997), other research points out that EVA does not dominate earnings in association with stock market returns (Dodd and Chen, 1996; Biddle *et al.*, 1997; Günther *et al.*, 1999). The implied effectiveness of EVA® as a performance measure based on the association between EVA® and stock return is therefore at least ambiguous.

Moreover, EVA®, being a single-period measure, does not address the problem of the time period over which profits are to be maximised (Grant, 1998) nor does it deal with issues about short-term horizons (McLaren, 2000). Furthermore, the EVA® practice of 'decoupling' performance measures from GAAP while having significant incentive benefits, also induces potential costs in the form of increased auditing requirements (Zimmerman in Minchington and Francis, 2000). Due to the fact that EVA® is a monetary measure, G. B. Stewart proposes standardising the metric on business unit level to reflect a common level of capital employed (Stewart, 1999; Morin and Jarrell, 2001). Finally, because EVA® assesses the capital charge on the firm's economic book value rather than on its market value, besides the fact that the adjusted capital only represents the values of the physical assets in place and not the strategy, some authors suggest using total market value of the firm's assets instead of the adjusted book value (Bacidore *et al.*, 1997).

Equity spread approach

The equity-spread approach is a future-oriented, accounting-based model. It compares return on equity (RoE) against the cost of equity

(k_E), and ascertains, by calculating the difference, if shareholder value has been created or destroyed. The equity spread approach is based on the Gordon model (Günther, 1997), which represents a market-to-book value relationship in efficient capital markets, under the assumption of unlimited constant growth (g) and with two other dependent variables: RoE and k_E. The market to book value can be calculated by dividing the difference between RoE and g, and k_E and g, when g is less than k_E:

$$\frac{M}{B} = \frac{(\text{RoE} - g)}{(k_E - g)} \quad \text{with } k_E > g$$

and

$$\frac{M}{B} = \begin{cases} +\infty & \text{if RoE} > g \\ 0 & \text{if RoE} = g \\ -\infty & \text{if RoE} < g \end{cases}$$

Market to book value ratios are well known and readily accepted among the financial scientific community (Günther, 1997). The consulting companies Marakon Associates and HOLT Value Associates have applied the approach in their value-based management practices. Although McTaggart suggests that the market to book equation should not be used to precisely estimate the value of a company, he asserts it can be used in three cases. Firstly, this ratio produces a meaningful quick and dirty valuation. Secondly, it draws out the key relationships between equity spread, growth and the ratio of market value to book value. And finally, the equation can be used to estimate a company's (or a business unit's) value at the end of the planning period (McTaggart et al., 1994).

The significant difference between both approaches is that in the EVA® approach economic value added is assessed by means of the weighted average cost of capital – and therefore considers both debt and equity – whereas the equity spread approach is interested only in the return against the cost of equity. The hurdle rate is therefore significantly different as it is recognised that the after-tax borrowing cost of debt is generally cheaper than the cost of equity (Pratt, 1998).

Multi-period metrics

Cash flow return on investment

We can define cash flow return on investment (CFROI) as the annual gross cash flow relative to the invested capital of the business unit (Lewis in Günther, 1997).

The mathematical formula for CFROI is the solution of r in:

$$I = \sum_{i=1}^{n} \frac{CF_i}{(1+r)^i} + \frac{W_{n+1}}{(1+r)^{n+1}}$$

where W = Expected residual value of non-depreciating assets, I = Gross operating asset investment and CF = Gross cash flow.

HOLT Value Associates, in co-operation with Boston Consulting Group, has developed CFROI. According to Haspeslagh *et al.* (2001), CFROI is quite popular; 23% of the respondents in their survey affirm their use of cash flow return on investment as an indicator for shareholder value creation.

The CFROI calculation requires four major inputs; the life of the assets; the amount of total assets (both depreciating and non-depreciating); the periodic cash flows assumed over the life of those assets; and the release of non-depreciating assets in the final period of the life of the assets (Madden, 1999; Young and O'Byrne, 2001; Morin and Jarrell, 2001). From a methodological point of view, CFROI can be determined in two steps (Myers, 1996). First, inflation-adjusted cash flows available to all capital owners in the firm are compared to the inflation-adjusted gross investments made by the capital owners. The ratio of gross cash flow to gross investment is translated into an internal rate of return by recognising the finite economic life of depreciating assets and the residual value of non-depreciating assets.

Madden (1998), a partner at HOLT Value Associates, cites a number of authors who claim that security analysts and corporate managers increasingly employ CFROI as a key tool for gauging corporate performance and shareholder value. Some of its users also perceive CFROI as an investor-oriented tool (Mills *et al.*, 1998). The CFROI model avoids the use of accounting book capital in valuing the firm's existing assets. Since the underlying gross cash flow for the calculation of CFROI is assumed to be constant during the useful life of the fixed assets (Morin and Jarrell, 2001), it is an annual performance figure that has to be re-calculated yearly (Günther, 1997; Young and O'Byrne, 2001). An often-heard comment with regard to CFROI is that it is perceived as a complex financial measure device (Fera, 1997; Young and O'Byrne, 2001).

Based on a simplified CFROI rate,[4] Boston Consulting Group developed a residual income measure, which is called cash value added

---

[4] In this approach CFROI is no longer calculated as the internal rate of return of a standardised gross cash flow profile but as gross cash flow minus economic depreciation, divided by gross investment.

(CVA). CVA is the spread between CFROI and the real cost of capital, multiplied by the investment in fixed assets plus working capital. Due to the fact that investors use analogous methods to value financial assets, CVA is seen as a consistent and relevant tool in communicating both internally and externally (Ottosen and Weissenrieder, 1996). In the above-mentioned study based on German Dax-100 companies, Günther et al. (1999) found that, although there was no evidence that one single performance measure perfectly explains capital market returns, CVA produces better results than the DCF approach or EVA®.

Shareholder value added

Shareholder value added (SVA) is defined as the difference between the present value of incremental cash flow before new investment and the present value of investment in fixed and working capital.

SVA = (Present value of cash flow from operations during the
       forecast period + Residual value + Marketable securities)
       − Debt

The measure has been described by Rappaport (1998) who is regarded as one of the most prominent publicists in the field of shareholder value metrics (Copeland et al., 2000; Günther, 1997). However, SVA is less popular than its founding father; only 8% of respondents in a recent INSEAD study (Boulos et al., 2001) confirm that they use this indicator.

SVA can also be defined as incremental sales multiplied by incremental threshold spread, adjusted for the income tax rate, divided by the present value of the cost of capital (Rappaport, 1998). Incremental threshold spread is calculated as the profit margin on incremental sales less the break-even operating profit margin on total sales in any period. In the latter means of representation, SVA leans towards the shareholder value network, which depicts the essential link between the corporate objective of creating shareholder value and the basic valuation or value drivers (Morin and Jarrell, 2001). The value driver model is a comprehensive approach that centres on seven key drivers of shareholder value; that is, sales growth rate, operating profit margin, cash tax rate, fixed capital needs, working capital needs, cost of capital and planning period or value growth duration (Rappaport, 1986). Compared with EVA®, Mills and Print (1995) express their preference in favour of SVA because the driver tree model appears to be very useful in helping managers to understand the dynamics of value creation. In a multi-divisional organisation the measurement of selected value drivers at the divisional level could be complementary to value-based measures at group level and eradicate the need to calculate divisional cost of capital.

4. VALUE-BASED MANAGEMENT PRACTICES

4.1. Introduction

In addition to the various performance indicators mentioned in the previous section, it should be clear that metrics are not the goal of a value-based management programme. As always, one should never confuse the ends with the means. Alas for some CEOs, a managing for value focus does not create value through financial manipulations. It merely creates value through developing sound strategic and operating plans for a company and its business units.

In this section we first introduce an overview of the fundamental components of a holistic value-based management programme. The components of this framework are deduced from several research reports concerning a comprehensive view of the practice of value-based management. We have set our framework beside the recently published INSEAD survey (Boulos *et al.*, 2001), *Getting the Value out of Value-Based Management*. In addition, we studied the results published in *Value-Based Management – The Growing Importance of Shareholder Value in Europe* (KPMG Consulting, 1999) and the conclusions of an inquiry elucidated in *Inside the Mind of the CEO in Belgium* (PricewaterhouseCoopers, 2000). We continue with an overview based on a literature review and analysis of what each of the consulting firms has published as its methodology. As stated earlier, value-based management as a practice emerged from the experience and fieldwork of professionals and consultants. We describe six of these value-based management constructs.

4.2. Value-based management in practice

Fieldwork by Boulos *et al.* (2001) concerning the VBM practice, reveals that a successful VBM programme is much more than the adoption of an economic profit metric as a key measure of performance. The authors conclude that a successful VBM programme is about introducing fundamental changes in the company's culture.

INSEAD's extensive research on value-based management (Boulos *et al.*, 2001) revealed the five key value-driven elements, described below. These five set up a virtuous circle of behaviour and benefits as a foundation for sustained value creation.

The first key element is an explicit commitment to value, which becomes apparent to everyone when a company sets shareholder goals to guide and expand upon thinking and actions. The education and intensive training of a large number of managers and employees in the shareholder value creation process and in the awareness of how their actions can contribute to economic profit creation, forms the second element. Building ownership is the third element mentioned; rewarding large numbers of managers and employees on corporate and/or business unit economic profit measures, has a positive influence on the creation of ownership. Empowering business units is the fourth main element; this empowerment concerns the evaluation of the strategic options and subsequent investment, based on the maximisation of the long-term economic-profit creation of the business unit. The fifth main element concerns broad process reforms. The most important rules concerning these broad programmes are: avoiding accounting complexity, identifying value, integrating budgeting with strategic planning and, last but not least, investing in information systems to develop an overall corporate strategy.

A correct implementation of these five key elements is necessary in order to benefit from VBM but, apart from this, the INSEAD survey (Boulos *et al.*, 2001) also specified some success factors that are indispensable in practice. Making the commitment to shareholder value explicit and providing intensive training for as many managers and employees as possible or desirable, are success factors situated at the beginning of the VBM implementation process. The involvement of the CEO is a success factor applied to the whole VBM practice. The extent of the bonus programme, the depolitisation of budgets and less frequent interventions in resource allocation programmes can be viewed as success factors, resulting from an adequate implementation and supporting the ongoing use of the VBM system.

Boulos *et al.* (2001) are, however, not the only people trying to explain the components or elements of a holistic value-based management system. Slater and Olson (1996) describe a comparable overview of the components in a VBM system. The first stage in their system consists of a value-based analysis. Such value-based analyses and planning techniques use several well-known financial tools, such as DCF and EVA®, to evaluate new strategic initiatives and existing operations. Like Boulos *et al.*, Slater and Olson subscribe to the need to involve all levels of management to achieve a successful VBM system. The commitment and support of top management is here the most important aspect, followed by the need to educate all other managers in order to create commitment in the whole organisation. According to Slater and Olson, the final step in this stage concerns the establishment of a clearly communicated gain-sharing programme for all employees and thus not exclusively for managers. More than Boulos *et al.*, Slater and Olson emphasise that the 'gain-sharing' programme can only be an effective motivational tool if the payout formula is clearly constructed. VBM training and open-book management are the key elements of the third stage in their VBM system. After this stage, everybody in the firm should understand the purpose of the VBM system, the mechanisms of the financial framework, the current financial situation and the benefits of achieving the firm's goals. The fourth stage focuses on employee empowerment and task-focused training, and the last stage concerns value sharing.

4.3. Value-based management as a practice

Numerous financial planning/consulting firms have developed proprietary theories of value creation (England, 1992). Each of them claims to have a specific presumption of how value can be managed. In this section we attempt to analyse their documented methodology. Table 4.1 provides a synopsis of the approach of six financial planning/consulting firms: Stern Stewart and Co; Marakon Associates; McKinsey and Co; PricewaterhouseCoopers; L.E.K. Consulting; and HOLT Value Associates. Before analysing the similarities and differences in their approaches, a brief description of each of the firms will be useful.

Stern Stewart and Co

Founded in 1982 (G. B. Stewart, 1999), this New York-based consulting firm is based on the development of its EVA® Management Framework. The EVA® and MVA metric (Günther, 1997; Myers, 1996), created internally, are probably the firm's best-known assets.

Marakon Associates

Founded in 1978 this management consulting firm was once depicted as the best-kept secret in consulting (T. A. Stewart, 1998). Marakon developed the equity spread metric (Günther, 1997; Reimann, 1991), which, as we have already mentioned, is rooted in the Gordon model. The firm's main interest in basically one governing objective, that is, the increase in shareholder value, explains its strong focus.

McKinsey & Co

This consulting firm (Copeland *et al.*, 2000) advises companies on general issues, such as strategy, but is also active in more specialised areas, including finance. The firm's ideas about value-based management are well elaborated in the book *Valuation, Measuring and Managing the Value of Companies*, where they pay a lot attention to the valuation metrics, and the DCF model in particular.

PricewaterhouseCoopers

PricewaterhouseCoopers has offices all over the world. Its global financial and cost management consultancy team (Read, 1997) is active in the field of planning and large-scale change projects by means of, for instance, value-based management (Table 4.1).

L.E.K. Consulting

Founded in 1983, L.E.K. provides its clients worldwide with strategic advice and commercial support. The prominent publicist in the field of shareholder value, Alfred Rappaport, has been L.E.K.'s strategic adviser concerning the application of shareholder value to business strategy since its merger with The Alcar Group in 1993.

HOLT Value Associates

The headquarters of HOLT are in Chicago (Young and O'Byrne, 2001). HOLT developed, in co-operation with the Boston Consulting Group (Günther, 1997; Myers, 1996), the CFROI-metric. The firm's expertise is mainly focused on understanding how companies, worldwide, are valued on stock markets (Madden, 1999).

Comparison of the VBM systems used by these different consulting firms reveals some similarities between the approaches, but also demonstrates clear distinctions and different accents.

Management focus

The six consulting companies all endorse and draw attention to the imperative of maximising shareholder value as the paramount performance objective.

The reason for shareholder value maximisation is, however, not univocal. McKinsey and Co (Copeland *et al.*, 2000), Pricewaterhouse-Coopers (Black *et al.*, 1998), L.E.K. Consulting (Rappaport, 1998) and HOLT Value Associates (Madden, 1999) refer to value-based management as a means to prosper in business. Stern Stewart and Co (Ehrbar, 1998; G. B. Stewart, 1999; Stern *et al.*, 2001) considers the recognition of ownership as the ultimate reason to maximise shareholder value. And for Marakon Associates (McTaggart and Kontes, 1993; McTaggart *et al.*, 1994; Miller, 2000) the *raison d'être* for VBM is the fact that it is deemed to be the best way to guarantee the going concern of the organisation.

Perception of the different stakeholders

There is clear unanimity with regard to the various stakeholder groups. All consulting companies in our assessment (Copeland, 1994; Read, 1997; Black *et al.*, 1998; Ehrbar, 1998; McTaggart and Gillis, 1998; Rappaport, 1998; G. B. Stewart, 1999; Madden, 1999; Copeland *et al.*, 2000; Stern *et al.*, 2001) agree that the interests of all stakeholder groups are best served when putting the shareholder first. Rappaport (1998) refers, therefore, as mentioned earlier, to the socially responsible behaviour of companies.

Fundamentals for value creation

Despite consensus on value creation and even value maximisation, there is a difference in the detail. Four of the six consultants – Marakon Associates, HOLT Value Associates, Stern Stewart and Co and L.E.K. Consulting – point to the importance of a well-founded strategy. One firm from this group, Marakon Associates, appears to focus predominantly on strategy. As indicated by McTaggart *et al.* (1994), a coherent strategy should allow companies to overcome both the internal force of constraints in the organisational structure or culture and the external force of competition in order to maximise shareholder value. Where HOLT Value Associates (Madden, 1999) combines strategy with metrics, Stern Stewart and Co (Stern *et al.*, 2001) incorporates strategy, structure and metrics, and refer to the 'Road Map to Value Creation' created by Briggs and Stratton.

   Although L.E.K. Consulting (Rappaport, 1998) shares the ideas of HOLT Value Associates concerning the combination of strategy and metrics as the fundamentals for value creation, there is a difference in emphasis. L.E.K. Consulting is aware of the importance of the shareholder value network as a metric framework, but stresses that shareholder value analysis is only as good as the strategic thinking behind it. Moreover, it not only recognises the importance of strategy but also puts a considerable amount of effort on the education part in their holistic approach.

   McKinsey and Co (Copeland *et al.*, 2000) also mentions metrics as one of the cornerstones of their system. Value metrics, together with a value mindset, which is denoted as the way management internalises the idea of shareholder value creation, are the two dimensions in value thinking. Copeland *et al.* consider value thinking as a prerequisite for making value happen.

   PricewaterhouseCoopers (Read, 1997) accentuates making the right structural decisions, and focuses on the challenge of streamlining the organisation on the one hand and the expansion of the organisation to serve customers worldwide, on the other.

Table 4.1 Comparison of six value-based management approaches.

	Stern Stewart & Co	Marakon Associates	McKinsey & Co	PricewaterhouseCoopers	L.E.K. Consulting	HOLT Value Associates
Management focus						
Why shareholder value maximisation?	Recognition of ownership	Best objective in going concern	Prosper in business	Prosper in business	Prosper in business	Prosper in business
	Successful companies maximise creation of wealth for the shareholders					
Philosophy of the consulting company with regards to stakeholder groups	Stakeholder theory, by means of putting the shareholder first					
Fundamentals for value creation	Strategy, structure and metrics	Strategy	Metrics and belief systems	Structure	Strategy and metrics	Strategy and metrics
Main elements in the consultants' approach	Systems with focus on measuring, training and rewarding	Culture, structure and systems with focus on decentralised strategy development	Culture, structure and systems with focus on corporate strategy and valuation	Culture, structure and systems with focus on training and communication	Culture and systems with focus on strategy and education	Systems with focus on valuation
Scope/Purpose of external communication concerning VBM	Better quality information Marketing advantage	Focus on wealth creation	Unequivocal information to all stakeholder groups	Better quality information Temporary marketing influences	Better quality information and commitment	Better quality information
Perception and specific (internal) contribution of the VBM and approach in general	Clarifies the perception of underlying economics	Better alignment of internal organisation and processes with strategy	Improving dialogue between different internal entities	Changing time-horizon and encouraging strategy development	Improving management productivity	More efficient analysis of firms' performance
Strategy development — General ideas	Overarching strategy and corresponding organisational structure	Bottom-up process Common framework Valuing strategies on profitable growth instead of growth	Decision-making at all levels Focus on valuing strategies	Common framework of corporate parent and business units Strategic thinking reconciled with financial thinking = 'Valuing strategies'	Strategic analysis at all levels based on combination of strategy formulation and strategy valuation	Strategy is induced by feedback from the stock market
Mentioned references	Refer to • Porter and Treacy & Wiersema for strategy development • Duncan & Brickley, Smith & Zimmerman for organisational design	Proprietary strategy approach, based on market economics and competitive position, resembles ideas of Porter	Refer to • Porter • Coyne & Subramaniam • Proprietary customer segmentation analysis • Competitive business system analysis	Briefly refer to Porter and Hamel & Prahalad for strategic thinking	Refer to • Porter for strategy formulation • Williams for the sustainability question Doubts about ideas of • Hammer & Champy • Hamel & Prahalad • Treacy & Wiersema	
Strategy deployment — General	Top-down, decentralised	Bottom-up, decentralised	Preference for bottom-up	Top-down and centralistic	Bottom-up with central guidance	Top
Focus in strategy deployment	Increasing EVA® as general objective	Profitable growth instead of growth per se	Profitable growth instead of growth per se	Maximisation of shareholder value	Maximisation of expected shareholder value added	
Supporting tools	EVA® value drivers, EVA® is common language for all management decisions	Strategic value drivers of different business units, benchmarked with corporate management processes, EP is common language	Key value drivers and key performance indicators defined separate for different organisational levels	Strategic value drivers are decomposed in financial value drivers and operational value drivers	Decomposition of the shareholder value network up to the level of key value drivers	
Preferred metrics	• MVA (corporate) • EVA® (corporate, business unit and product line)	• Equity spread (corporate) • EP (corporate, business unit, customer and product line)	• Enterprise DCF (corporate, business unit) • EP (corporate, business unit, customer and product line)	• CFROI (corporate) • SVA (corporate, business unit) • FCF (corporate, business unit)	• SVA (corporate, operating level) • Change in residual income or change in EVA® (operating level) • Leading indicators of value (operating level)	• CFROI (corporate) • Accounting-based measures (lower levels)
Investment decisions and resource allocation	Valuation of strategies based on EVA® valuation	Focus on fulfilment of strategy requirements of the business unit Four principles for resource allocation	Focus on valuation techniques: • DCF • Real option theory	Focus on maximisation of SHV and alignment with strategy	Focus on market signals analysis combined with DCF and real options as valuation tools	DCF in two parts; existing assets versus future investments

Mergers and acquisitions		EVA® analysis combined with strategic considerations	Develop an acquisition strategy	Discipline acquisition programme	Structured approach combined with common sense	Discipline acquisition process	CFROI analysis
Influence on collaboration		Dynamic discussions at steering committee Commonality across processes and measures	Creation of 'managing for value' mindset	Aligning BU managers and employees around a common understanding of top priorities	Bridging corporate and frontline managers' strategy and its implementation	Aligning managers with a common framework of analysis, a common goal and common language	Create common language, continuous improvement through feedback system
Performance management	Performance management	Paramount objective is increasing EVA® EVA® is internalised through cross-functional teams Preference for EVA® valuation model and free cash flow model	Suggested process consists of three activities: • Target setting • Monitoring performance • Examine difference Two principles: • Plan-driven targets • Performance contracts	Prescribed system contains three elements: • Value creation strategy for business units • Alignment between targets and value drivers at every level • Structured performance review Four principles: • Tailor-made • Long- and short-term targets • Financial and operational targets • Leading indicators	Proposed system is based on four elements: • Target setting • Linking goals to value drivers on lower level • Define micro-drivers • Value chain analysis	Focus on development of an organisation-wide 'owner-oriented culture' Installation of more ownership-oriented perspective consists of three steps: • Overcome earnings myopia • Measure and reward long-term performance • Convey risks and rewards of ownership Performance measurement hierarchy Shareholder value network	Focus on learning process (not elaborated) At lower levels switch to simpler accounting-based tools
		Resemblance to the shareholder value network of Rappaport (1986)	Proposed strategy is validated (projections of revenue growth, EP and Equity CF) and once approved it becomes the target	Resemblance to the shareholder value network of Rappaport (1986)	Resemblance to the shareholder value network of Rappaport (1986)		
	Target setting	EVA® goals as basis for stretched targets		Iterative process (negotiation between different organisational levels)	Translate global targets to localised targets at operational level	Translate shareholder returns at corporate level to specific key value drivers on the lowest organisational level	CFROI goals (at higher levels) translated in more local targets
Reward system	Basis for rewarding	Link rewards to value creation	Link rewards to performance consistent with value creation	Link individuals' behaviour to overall value-creating activities	Link rewards to value creation	Compensation based on superior performance (Sustainable Shareholder Value Added, SSVA™)	Compensation based on an empirical link to value
	General ideas	Putting executives at the same risk as stockholders Start with top management and gradually extend through the ranks of middle management	Alignment between top management and governing objective Focus on top management	Making managers think like owners All employees throughout the organisation	Appropriate level of risk and reward All employees throughout the organisation	Acquire experience and understanding with the shareholder value approach first, before linking to remuneration All employees throughout the organisation	Acquire experience with the CFROI model first, before linking to remuneration
	Key elements	Results and not performance is rewarded Features of rewarding system (= bonus bank): • Based on EVA® measure • Unambiguous target • Uncapped bonuses • Based on improvement on corresponding level • Stretching horizon from short term to longer term	Economic performance as basis Features of rewarding system: • First focus on the right strategies and organisational capabilities then on financial rewards • One corporate performance target, tailored targets for the business unit based on its strategy • Targets are defined in contract • Compensation on one-year results • Performance on corresponding level as basis for rewarding • Relative pay for relative performance • Linked short- and long-term targets	Individual behaviour and performance as basis for rewarding Features of rewarding system: • Challenging financial and non-financial targets • Linked long- and short-term targets • Aversion against bonus caps • Corresponding performance • Targets tailored for different levels and linked to controllable Key Performance Indicators (KPIs) • Visualise realised performance • Differentiate rewarding	Basis is economic performance Features of rewarding system: • Linked with strategy • Separate long- and short-term targets • Depending on hierarchy level • Related to responsibilities • Subscribe to the idea of long-term incentive plans	Exceeding the threshold standard for superior performance as basis Features of rewarding system: • Based on SVA measure • Based on improvement on corresponding level • Linked short- and long-term targets • One corporate performance target, tailored targets for lower organisational levels • Aversion against bonus caps • Related to responsibilities • Compensation on rolling three- to five-year SVA plans • Subscribe to bonus-bank approach • Relative pay for relative performance	
		Cash rewarding combined with internal rewarding Encourage employee stock ownership	Individual payment choice (cash or cash equivalents, options)	Financial incentives fulfilled with opportunities, values and beliefs form the reward package		Indexed stock options Encouragement of stock ownership or stock options	

(continued)

Table 4.1 (cont.)

		Stern Stewart & Co	Marakon Associates	McKinsey & Co	PricewaterhouseCoopers	L.E.K. Consulting	HOLT Value Associates
Training and education	General ideas	Changing the mindset; Continuous communication with entire workforce; Top-down	'Learn by doing'; Continuous reinforcement through top management communication; Top-down to all levels	First, survey managers anonymously about beliefs and values, before changing beliefs and values; Entire organisation	Value transformation team educates management and business units; Endorsement from top to all employees	Continuous education; 'Train the trainers' approach; Shareholder Value Education Agenda; Endorsement from top to all employees	
	Content	Focus on EVA®	Focus on developing and implementing strategies that maximise governing objective	Emphasis on value creation	Focus on share price goal – shareholder value theme	Focus on superior total shareholder return (SSVA™)	
Facilitators for the implementation of the VBM approach		Installation of steering committee; Commitment of CEO and CFO; Formal implementation team; Regular meeting with consulting firm to continue knowledge transfer	Chief executive as visible leader; Top management champions to drive implementation	Visible top management commitment; Extensive participation of business unit managers in value driver analysis	CEO sponsorship, with support of senior management and board of directors; Value transformation team, consisting of representatives of all levels	CEO commitment, with full support of the Board and management; Various facilitating constructs	
Benchmarking	Corporate level	Compare sum of EVA®'s of business plans with market value of company	Compare key management processes	DCF	Cash flow performance compared with competing companies; Board definition of benchmarking	Relative total shareholder return or comparing company's total return with a group of comparable peers; DCF when absence of true current market benchmark	Compare forecast patterns with historical information
	Business unit level	EVA® drivers to compare internal	Identification of strategic value drivers	DCF combined with EP to benchmark	Business unit-lspecific value driver	Business unit's operating plan; Historical performance of the business unit; Competitive performance of value drivers; Market expectations for the whole company; DCF when absence of true current market benchmark	NCR drivers

Main elements of the consultants' approaches

The main elements of the approaches of all consultant companies, with the exception of Stern Stewart and Co (Stern *et al.*, 2001) and HOLT Value Associates (Madden, 1998), show clear similarities with the basic mechanisms of a management control system defined by Anthony and Govindarajan (2001) as culture, structure and systems. We found, however, a distinctive emphasis in each of the four approaches.

The decentralisation of strategy development substantiates the focus of Marakon Associates. The Marakon practitioners are first of all centred on belief systems, which imbue an organisation with a sense of purpose and a basis for decision-making. The next element concerns the principles, defined as the knowledge and guidelines for decision-making. Within this framework of beliefs and principles, the institutional capability to manage effectively is provided by the processes (McTaggart *et al.*, 1994). The valuation framework of McKinsey and Co (Copeland *et al.*, 2000) is built on the same mechanisms but with a different focus. The McKinsey approach emphasises corporate strategy and includes identifying and making an inventory of the value creation situation, acting on opportunities – that often involve reorganisation or divestures and acquisitions – and implementing a value creation philosophy. Even more than McKinsey, HOLT's model of shareholder value management focuses on valuation and expressing the link between strategy deployment and the way in which stock markets value companies. The approach of HOLT Value Associates, which is said to be comprehensive and complex (Reimann, 1991), includes an economic framework combined with attention for corporate vision and strategic business unit strategy.

According to PricewaterhouseCoopers (Black *et al.*, 1998), the shareholder value methodology is based on a triple transformation process. The first step is called analysis. It is the learning process of linking strategy to operations on the one hand and the effect of value drivers on both operations and strategy on the other. The second step defined as action, is the transformation of people, culture and other stakeholders in order to build long-term sustainable value. Finally, internal and external communication completes this three-stage process. Black *et al.* suggest accomplishing this process with another three-stage concept including value creation, value preservation and value realisation. The attention for training and communication in both processes demonstrates their importance in the PricewaterhouseCoopers approach.

L.E.K. Consulting (Rappaport, 1998) also distinguishes three major phases in its implementation process of the shareholder value approach. The first phase focuses on gaining commitment. In this way, the L.E.K. team underlines the importance of creating consensus on the need to change, not only at senior level, but on a much broader organisational level. The second phase, introducing shareholder value, consists of creating an understanding of how to change, based on different techniques, that is, value audit, value driver assessment, strategy valuation and shareholder value education. Reinforcing shareholder value is the third and last phase in the L.E.K. approach and focuses on ensuring that the change is sustained. Performance measurement and incentives, shareholder value infrastructure and continuing education are the suggested management processes to keep shareholder value thinking alive.

As mentioned above, the approach of Stern Stewart and Co (Stern *et al.*, 2001) differs noticeably from the frameworks of the other consulting firms in that its own integrated EVA programme is basically oriented towards systems and consists of a measurement programme, combined with a management system, an incentive compensation plan and training.

External communication

None of the six consulting firms denies the importance or impact of external communication with regard to value-based management. However, it seems they do not have the same opinion about the specific scope and purpose of external communication.

Stern Stewart and Co, as well as PricewaterhouseCoopers, HOLT Value Associates and L.E.K. Consulting, aim to provide the investment community with better quality information. Madden (1999) thereby refers to the usefulness of this information for the decision-making process of the investors, on resource allocation and investment decisions. According to PricewaterhouseCoopers, investor communication is essential to ensure that investors understand the company's goals and strategies and that they are confident about the ability of management to implement and deliver those objectives. Like Stern Stewart and Co, PricewaterhouseCoopers is, as we will illustrate below, aware of the influence of this communication as a marketing tool, but Pricewaterhouse-Coopers particularly emphasises that these influences are only temporary and are difficult to sustain.

L.E.K. Consulting is also very concerned about the alignment between the market evaluation and the company's strategic plans. This concern about providing investors with accurate information resulted in the publication of *The Shareholder Scoreboard*. This annual publication focuses on rate of return rankings for the 1,000 largest companies in the United States. Rappaport, as mentioned above, starts out with the company's stock price as the clearest measure of market expectations (Rappaport, 1987; Rappaport, Vol. V; Rappaport, 1998). Needless to say, this consulting firm pays special attention to these market expectations. By means of a Market Signals Analysis process, L.E.K. Consulting tries to demystify the expectations or signals from analysts with both a buying and selling focus and consequently forms the basis for proactive initiatives regarding communication with the market or valuation adjustments (Kenney, Vol. IX). Since the approach of L.E.K. Consulting is entirely built upon superior total shareholder returns, this not only sends unambiguous signals to members of the organisation but also to outside investors. After all, a focus on superior total shareholder returns assures the owners of a firm that management is totally committed to exceeding peer shareholder returns performance (Rhoads, Vol. X).

According to Stern *et al.* (2001), the EVA® framework is a superior instrument for investors who are interested in the reality behind the accounting numbers. G. B. Stewart (1999) and Young and O'Byrne (2001) are also deceptively confident of the added value of EVA® in external communications. And G. B. Stewart thereby underlines the importance of EVA® in communication with the most influential investors or lead steers. Stern Stewart and Co (Stern *et al.*, 2001) recognises the impact of the announcement of the implementation of EVA® on the perception of the lead steers; not only the transmission of data, but also the announcement of implementation of EVA® can influence investors since this information is often seen as a way of creating more confidence in the company's future performance.

Marakon Associates (McTaggart *et al.*, 1994) advocates the importance of communicating nothing more or nothing less than the amount of wealth the company will create for its shareholders. According to McKinsey and Co (Copeland *et al.*, 2000), companies should apply the same communication strategy for internal and external communication. Copeland *et al.* suggest treating investors, investment community, customers and employees all with the same assiduousness.

Internal contribution of the VBM approach

The perception of the internal contribution of the VBM approach seems to be closely linked with communication, since all six consulting firms denote in one way or another its influence on internal communication. Stern Stewart and Co (Ehrbar, 1998) define the EVA® framework as a new perspective that provides managers with a clearer perception of the underlying economics of the business. Madden (1999) is on the same wavelength as Stern Stewart and Co in that he specifies a more efficient analysis of the firms' performance as one of the main contributions of value-based management.

McTaggart *et al.* (1994) stress the increase in alignment of the internal organisation and processes with the (corporate) strategy. McKinsey and Co (Copeland *et al.*, 2000) refers mainly to the improvement of the dialogue between corporate and business unit level. Read (1997), the global leader of PricewaterhouseCoopers's Financial and Cost Management team, is convinced that implementing VBM can change people's time horizon and motivation to achieve the corporate goals. Rappaport (1998) summarises the internal contribution of implementing the shareholder value approach as an improvement of management productivity by facilitating more efficient and effective decision-making. Smith (Vol. XIV), a partner in L.E.K.'s London office, thereby distinguishes three categories of features. First: the systematic way of collecting and evaluating operating measures that control and drive cash flow. Second: Smith emphasises that strategic decisions are made on the basis of a systematic analysis of potential value creation. Third: the fact that employees at all levels understand how their activities link to the creation of short- and long-term cash flow (Roath, Vol. IV).

Strategy development

There are some distinct differences in the recommended strategy development process of the various consultants. The approach of HOLT Value Associates (Madden, 1999) can be considered here as the exception, since Madden states that strategy is induced by feedback from the stock market due to early recognition of fundamental changes.

Stern Stewart and Co (Stern *et al.*, 2001) has, notwithstanding the lack of an own strategy approach, a clear view on strategy development and admit that the existence of an EVA® framework is not sufficient to be successful. Stern *et al.* recognise the need of an all-embracing strategy combined with an organisational structure that supports the chosen strategy. The identification of the appropriate competitive position based on Porter's competitive advantage is seen as the basic principle in the strategy development process, and the allocation of the key resources as described by Treacy and Wiersema, can be viewed as the most important strategic element. The approaches of Duncan and Brickley, Smith and Zimmerman are considered to be an excellent basis to resolve the questions related to structural design. Possibly due to Stewart's background as a corporate financier, Stern Stewart & Co also cultivates capital structure and deployment of capital (Young and O'Byrne, 2001) as a major element in the strategic process.

Marakon Associates (McTaggart *et al.*, 1994) has developed a universal framework for strategy development. It envisions this strategic planning process as a primary decision-making tool. The Marakon framework is based on three characteristics. First of all, it needs to be value based. Secondly, it is important that the process is consequential, which implies that the major business units and appropriate decisions determine short- and long-term performance. The third characteristic refers to continuity, where important issues are constantly under assessment and discussion. The strategy development process is a 'bottom-up' process to assure an accurate appraisal of the various business units in the portfolio. The financial forecasts, developed by the business units, are hereby supposed to be underpinned by means of an extensive analysis of market economics and competitive position. This approach (Brown *et al.*, 2000), as described by McTaggart *et al.* (1994), reveals great similarities with Porter's Industry Structure Analysis.[5]

Porter also plays a very important role in the strategy development approach of L.E.K. Consulting. This provider of financial planning services distinguishes two activities in the strategic analysis of any business. The first activity, defined as strategy formulation, entails analysing the attractiveness of the industry and the position of the business *vis-à-vis* its competitors. The second activity, strategy valuation, involves an estimation of the shareholder value added by alternative strategies (Rappaport, 1981; 1998; Rhoads, Vol. X). Rappaport (1998) takes a clear standpoint concerning the availability of systematic frameworks for strategy formulation, since he states that only the Five Forces Model of Porter and the Strengths/Weaknesses/Opportunities/Threats analyses succeed in linking the investigation of industry attractiveness and the sources of competitive advantage with shareholder value. He continues to argue in favour of Porter by expressing his doubts on the approaches of Hammer & Champy, Hamel & Prahalad and Treacy & Wiersema, which, according to him, do not succeed in explaining how those recommended strategies will lead to significant increases in shareholder value. It is not only important to detect competitive advantages, but it is also important to sustain those advantages. Rappaport refers therefore to Williams and his classification of products and services into three categories, based on the sustainability of the competitive advantage: slow cycle, standard cycle and fast cycle. The strategy development approach suggested by L.E.K. Consulting continues with a translation of these competitive dynamics into financial drivers. The alternative strategies for gaining competitive advantage form the basic inputs for the strategy valuation process, where Rappaport distinguishes two phases. The first phase focuses on establishing

---

[5] Often referred to as the Five Forces Model.

reasonable forecasts, while the second evaluates the resulting valuations (Rappaport, 1981; 1992; 1998).

One of the partners of McKinsey & Co (Koller, 1994) is an adherent of decision-making at all levels, on condition that everyone is provided with accurate information and proper incentives. The business unit strategy is not viewed as part of the valuation process, but as a prerequisite for effective business performance management. Not only Stern Stewart & Co, Marakon Associates and L.E.K. Consulting but also McKinsey & Co (Copeland *et al.*, 2000) propose to use Porter's Five Forces Model as a means of developing the strategic perspective. Copeland *et al.* furthermore denote the customer segmentation analysis, the competitive business system analysis and the Coyne/Subramaniam Industry Model as useful analytical frameworks to underpin the strategic perspective. Another important element (Copeland *et al.*, 2000) in the strategy development process of McKinsey and Co concerns scenario-planning. Copeland *et al.* concur that it is more appropriate to investigate different scenarios than to build only one most likely forecast.

Black *et al.* (1998) state that the adoption of shareholder value as a standard creates a common framework that provides better decision-making at all levels. The valuation of strategies does not only involve strategic thinking, based on the ideas of Porter and Hamel and Prahalad, but also incorporates financial consideration in the process.

Strategy deployment

Increasing EVA® is recommended (G. B. Stewart, 1999) as the overriding objective in the approach of Stern Stewart & Co and should therefore be considered as the basis for decision-making at every hierarchical level. Despite the need to standardise EVA® when used at business unit level, the EVA® financial management system provides a common language for everyone in the organisation. The use of this framework is supposed to minimise the subjective debates during the evaluation of alternative business strategies and financial structures. EVA® value drivers (Young and O'Byrne, 2001) explain the creation or destruction of value and trace the sources back to individual financial and non-financial performance variables at the corporate and business unit level.

Marakon Associates (McTaggart *et al.*, 1994; Armour and Mankins, 2001) describes great benefits in a grounded appraisal of business units, combined with a chief executive who is engaged in the approval of the strategies on the various levels. It considers the corporate level of the organisation as the challenger and the founder, whereas the business units are seen as the entrepreneurs. This explains the opinion of McTaggart *et al.* (1994) that companies need two separate, but related planning processes: one at the corporate and one at the business unit level. Strategic planning then becomes a bottom-up process, supported (Armour and Mankins, 2001) by a clear decision-making authority and explicit accountability for financial performance. Detailed financial and strategic information is essential to determine opportunities and fulfil the requirements at business unit level, and forms the basis for developing and evaluating strategic options. This strategic assessment is said to be very helpful to obtain the best information on the sources and drivers for value. It allows business units to identify the strategic value drivers controllable for that specific business unit and in this way contributes directly to the consolidation at corporate level. Marakon Associates distinguishes three components in the strategic analysis at business unit level. The strategic and the financial characterisation of different products and customer segments are the first two components, whereas the major influences of these characterisations on the major sources and drivers of value creation and destruction, under the current strategy of those units, form the third one.

Not only Marakon Associates but also Koller (1994) believes that a top down command and control structure is not the most appropriate way for strategy deployment, certainly not in large multi-business organisations. This view is in line with the perception of Copeland *et al.* (2000) that top-level decision-making requires extensive understanding of the elements in the day-to-day operations of the organisation. McKinsey & Co (Koller, 1994; Copeland *et al.*, 2000) names these variables key value drivers and state that they are useful at the generic, business unit and operational level. The following step in the strategy deployment process concerns the definition of the key performance indicators (KPIs), the related metrics for the value drivers. In order to put sufficient emphasis on profitable growth, Copeland *et al.* advise combining the use of value drivers with a growth horizon analysis to make sure that the company has a balanced view of the potential sources of value creation.

Smith (Vol. XIV) also distinguishes problems in a top-down approach for strategy deployment, but his concern focuses on the creation of ownership. He states that, without underestimating the importance of corporate ownership and the support of the CEO, objectives developed at corporate level can cause a lot of buy-in problems at the lower business unit levels. To overcome the various potential problems with conventional planning, he suggests selecting either Intensive Strategy Analysis or Issue-Driven Strategic Planning for strategic planning at business unit level. However, this does not mean that corporate planning is only useful at corporate level. Roads and Goulding (Vol. XVII) summarise the different roles of corporate planning by saying that it is first of all used to conduct corporate level planning. Furthermore, it can facilitate Strategic Business

Unit (SBU) level planning and align business function plans. They continue by stating that corporate planning has a unique position to increase the value of cross-business synergies, align SBU planning efforts and business function plans with corporate objectives. According to them, it depends on the level of diversity and centralisation on the businesses whether the planning function is more an active participant or either a facilitator to business unit planning. They prefer planning at the group level when potential synergies between business units can be exploited. Notwithstanding the fact that each level has different strategic tasks, it remains important that they are all linked by the one common objective to create shareholder value.

The shareholder value network, created by Rappaport, occupies a prominent position in the shareholder value approach of L.E.K. Consulting. This network depicts the essential link between the corporate objective of creating shareholder value and the basic valuation parameters or value drivers. Rappaport distinguishes seven value drivers in his network. Each of those value drivers contributes to one of the three valuation components – cash flow from operations, discount rate and debt – that, in their turn, influence the corporate objective. Three of the seven value drivers – sales growth, operating profit margin and income tax rate – are influenced by the operating decisions of management. Working capital investment and fixed capital investment, two other value drivers, are governed by the investment decisions of management. The financing decisions of management influence the sixth value driver, cost of capital. The value growth duration is the seventh and last value driver in the shareholder value network and is, according to Rappaport, management's best estimate of the number of years that investments can be expected to yield rates of return higher than the cost of capital. The key value driver analysis, sometimes referred to as the value driver mapping process, is furthermore recommended for the identification of the corresponding value drivers on the diverse organisational levels (Rappaport, 1998; Schor, Vol. I).

Since PricewaterhouseCoopers (Black *et al.*, 1998) subscribes to the vision that the different hierarchical levels make different kinds of decisions, it is not surprising that they stress the need to make everybody aware of VBM principles, with a focus on the maximisation of shareholder value. The strategic matters, like market selection, are questions for the chairman, the CEO and the CFO. Capital expenditure and investment questions need to be addressed in the strategic business units. Finally, detailed planning and budgeting are concerns at business unit level. Targets are deployed in a top-down mode. After global target setting, based on corporate analysis and share price objectives, it is suggested that these targets be translated into more localised and achievable goals at the operating level. Consequently, the impacts of these operational targets on generic financial value drivers on the common planning plat-form are assessed. The final step is the determination of a clear link between the operational drivers, measured by business-specific measures and the financial value drivers.

Madden (1999) refers to the advantages of the CFROI valuation map within the strategy development framework. This map allows for identify-ing and locating major value determinants and is primarily useful at corporate level. Managers at lower organisational levels are challenged to translate the accounting-based tools that help to improve business processes that drive these accounting results.

Preferred metrics

As mentioned above, there is a wide range of measures available to establish the value of organisations or determine whether or not an organisational unit has contributed to the overall value-maximising objective. Our research reveals that each of the considered professional service firms more or less has a tendency towards using specific value-based measures.

Stern Stewart & Co suggests combining the use of EVA® and MVA. Stern *et al.* (2001) as well as Young and O'Byrne (2001) define the first measure as the prime indicator of shareholder value. This results, accord-ing to the firm, in an excellent measurement system, since it is not only very useful at corporate ranks but can be broken down to whatever level: the level of a division, a factory, a store or even a product line. The successful deployment of the EVA® measure in the organisation depends on three factors (Stern *et al.*, 2001): the commitment of the chief executive to support the use of EVA® at lower levels in the company, the link with an incentive programme and the degree to which measurement makes sense at the various levels. Ehrbar (1998) completes the list of alleged advantages with three other benefits. The first refers to the fact that EVA® makes managers aware of the cost of capital and encourages them to reject investments with returns lower than the cost of capital. Subsequently, Ehrbar also mentions the adjust-ments to conventional accounting as a benefit. The third advantage is the direct link of EVA® with MVA (G. B. Stewart, 1999).

SVA is, in the approach of L.E.K. Consulting, defined as the ultimate measure, not only at corporate level but also at operating level. Two other measures, the change in EVA® and the change in residual income, are regarded as excellent alternatives. Although Rappaport (1998; Vol. V) admits that only the multiplication with the cost of capital is the differ-entiating factor between SVA and the change in residual income or EVA®, SVA remains for him the best estimate of change in value (Rhoads, Vol. X).

Only the difference in gaining acceptance and thus increasing the chances of successful implementation is, for him, an overriding factor to select the change in residual income or the change in EVA instead of SVA. However, L.E.K. Consulting realises that these measures are not specific and accountable enough for operating management and therefore recommends companies to focus on the key value drivers at the corresponding operating levels. These value drivers, at a specific operating level, have two characteristics. They are, first of all, the factors that have a significant value impact on that operating level and thus on the creation of value at corporate level. And secondly, the value drivers are controllable factors at the corresponding operating level (Rappaport, 1998; Schor, Vol. I).

The preferred measures of Marakon Associates (McTaggart *et al.*, 1994; McTaggart and Gillis, 1998) are equity spread, employed at company level, and economic profit, not only applicable at corporate level, but also at business unit level, the level of a customer or a product. The fact that economic profit is a single monetary measure, easy to link to value creation and that it is an easy measure to understand for non-financial managers, are the two major advantages of economic profit cited by McTaggart *et al.* (1994).

McKinsey & Co (Copeland *et al.*, 2000) advises the economic profit model and the enterprise DCF model as frameworks to evaluate businesses and understand the drivers of value creation. The economic profit model is a single period metric, where the enterprise DCF model is defined as a CFROI metric and valid for multi-business companies. Madden (1999) focuses primarily on the measurement on corporate level, based on CFROI.

Black *et al.* (1998) particularly draw attention to the assumption that all metrics are based on a common economic foundation. They agree, however, that each of the metrics can play a significant role in the value creation process. Business unit and corporate performance are best captured with the economic profit-metric. The CFROI-metric is suggested to evaluate long-term strategy and resource allocation. Finally, PricewaterhouseCoopers advises using the free cash flow model to study the link between strategic and operational objectives on the one hand and the goal of maximising value on the other hand.

Investment decision and resource allocation

Closely related to the strategy development process is the matter of investment decision and resource allocation. It is therefore not surprising that none of the consultants avoid this topic during their description of the proposed strategy development process. In their analysis of the strategy development and strategy deployment process, Stern Stewart & Co (G. B. Stewart, 1999; Ehrbar, 1998) mainly focuses on EVA® for decision-making and resource allocation. EVA® is seen as the ideal instrument to create a common language and to avoid endless subjective discussions, based on the use of vague investment and resource allocation decision criteria. Comparing the EVA® results of alternative strategies is assumed to give managers chance to identify underperforming variables and to look for improvements.

The policy of Marakon Associates (McTaggart *et al.*, 1994) with regard to investments is based on the idea that capital resources are allocated to business units and not between them. Every business unit can obtain as much capital as needed, provided that the proposed strategies contribute to the corporate governing objective. Marakon Associates establishes four principles for resource allocation. The zero-based idea of resource allocation is the first principle. The second principle deals with the fact that management should fund strategies instead of projects. Zero-tolerance in case of non-productive resource usage and the assumption that there is no capital rationing, substantiate the final two principles. Marakon Associates and PricewaterhouseCoopers (Black *et al*, 1998) equally stress the need to execute only those investment decisions that are in harmony with the corporate strategy and the objective of share-holder maximisation. Since these decisions are made at the strategic business unit level, they emphasise again that a thorough understanding of the value creating elements is indispensable.

McKinsey & Co (Copeland *et al.*, 2000) suggests two techniques for the valuation of investment decisions, traditional DCF methods and real options. They remark that the second valuation technique is preferable in situations with significant future flexibility.

The approach of L.E.K. Consulting concerning investment decisions and resource allocation integrates the main ideas of Marakon Associates, PricewaterhouseCoopers and McKinsey & Co. The idea that operating managers need to assess the value creation potential of alternative strategies forms the prerequisite in this approach. In several of his publications Rappaport (1987; 1990) uses the statement of Marakon Associates that managers should invest in strategies and not in projects. Although the partners of L.E.K. Consulting are aware of the distinction between corporate return and shareholder return, they underline the importance of corporate return in the decision-making process. And, although it is essential that the return on investments exceeds the cost of capital, they do not underestimate the importance of a return that exceeds the expectations of the shareholders, since they are convinced of the positive effects of an effective hurdle rate on management behaviour. As a result, they support the establishment of a hurdle rate that takes into consideration the market expectations as well (Rappaport, 1999). As described earlier, the market signals' analysis is for them the most apt instrument to gain some insight in the market expectations. Concerning the metrics, they share the opinion of McKinsey & Co when it expresses the importance of combining the standard DCF valuation with the most suitable real option approach. Another important point in their ideas on investment decisions and resource allocation is the recommendation to use not just one company-wide hurdle rate, but to link the hurdle rate with the specific characteristics of an investment.

According to Madden (1999), the CFROI model of HOLT Value Associates is a workable method for investment decisions since the net cash return is separated into two parts, of which the first one is related to the existing assets and the second one refers to future investments. This approach gives decision-makers the chance to check on the value of future investments and allows them to make better resource allocation and investment decisions. The availability of the long-term series of CFROIs, together with a relative wealth index, gives managers the chance to make more accurate predictions of the returns on new investments.

Mergers and acquisitions

Since the mergers and acquisitions issue can be considered as a specific kind of investment decision, it is not surprising that the proposed approaches of our six firms towards this issue bear a likeness to their ideas on investment decisions. Stern Stewart & Co and HOLT Value Associates draw attention to their previously described metrics model. The EVA® framework (Ehrbar, 1998; G. B. Stewart, 1999; Stern *et al.*, 2001) is again put forward by Stern Stewart & Co. Ehrbar illustrates the fact that EVA® is a powerful tool for strategic planning and decision-making with the example of an acquisition candidate. He describes how managers can value an acquisition candidate by evaluation of the contribution of this potential acquisition to EVA®. Stern *et al.* endorse the perception of Ehrbar, but remark that an EVA® analysis does not take into account the non-financial implications of an acquisition. This shortcoming can be set off if the decision-makers also consider the strategic implications of the potential acquisitions. G. B. Stewart suggests using the value-driver model for the valuation of the acquisitions benefits. HOLT Value Associates (Madden, 1999) emphasises that its CFROI model is suitable for every valuation issue, in which accuracy is essential. It is thus not surprising that it mentions this model as the most suitable for acquisition pricing.

Marakon Associates (McTaggart *et al.*, 1994) encourages companies to develop their own acquisition strategy. This strategy will guide management in their search for acquisition candidates who seem more valuable for their own shareholders than for the shareholders of the seller.

Copeland *et al.* (2000) have learned by experience to be careful with acquisitions, as they noticed that numerous corporate acquisitions had a negative influence on the acquiring shareholders. They developed a disciplined acquisition plan, based on the results of their research on the most common failures in acquisitions and the factors guaranteeing successful acquisitions. The disciplined acquisition plan consists of five steps; the first is a pre-acquisition phase, in which their own company and the industries are examined. This step is followed by the identification and screening of possible candidates. The assessment of high potential candidates forms the third step. After the negotiation and contract phase, the process ends with a carefully planned post-merger integration.

There are many analogies between the ideas of McKinsey & Co and L.E.K. Consulting concerning mergers and acquisitions. In his article in the *Harvard Business Review* in 1979, Rappaport drew attention to the advantages of using a market signals analysis. He made a distinction between three phases in the process of analysing acquisitions: planning; search and screen; and financial evaluation. The importance of a well-defined acquisition process was again emphasised in more recent publications by Rappaport himself and several other partners of L.E.K. Consulting (Rappaport, 1987; 1990; 1998; Kozin, Vol. III). In *Creating Shareholder Value*, Rappaport extended the three earlier mentioned stages with two additional ones. These stages are quite similar to those recognised by McKinsey. According to Rappaport (1998), one should start with a competitive analysis followed by a search and screen phase. After these steps, management should have a look at some strategy development issues completed with a financial evaluation, to conclude with the negotiating phase. Since mergers and acquisitions are seen as a specific sort of investment decision by L.E.K. Consulting, just like most of the others, it is not surprising that it recommends taking the previously described recommendations into account.

Not only McKinsey & Co. and L.E.K. Consulting but also PricewaterhouseCoopers (Black *et al.*, 1998) advise caution when acquisition options are evaluated. This explains why it developed a framework for best practice in acquisitions. The link to shareholder value is the leitmotiv throughout their framework, defined as a simplified transaction map. This transaction map can be subdivided into three main groups: the determination of the initial value and the resources used, the detection of possible synergies, and the financial engineering aspect. PricewaterhouseCoopers is however aware of the restrictions of this structured approach and therefore recommends using this transaction map in combination with common sense.

Influence on collaboration

Closely related to the impact of value-based management on both external and internal communication, is the influence on collaboration. The famous statement by Stern Stewart & Co (G. B. Stewart, 1999): 'Making managers into owners' immediately indicates their tendency in thinking towards collaboration. EVA® is not only viewed as a measurement instrument but is also an appropriate instrument to align the interests of managers and stakeholders and to encourage everyone to work together to realise the objectives of the shareholders (Stern et al., 2001). Using the EVA® financial management system (Ehrbar, 1998) and thus focusing on EVA® as the only measure to pursue value, reduces conflicts and confusion in the organisation and simplifies decision-making. EVA® (Stern et al., 2001) guides not only lower organisational levels, it is also an important instrument for the steering committee, when discussing the way of organising the collaboration, in order to consolidate the presupposed EVA® targets. Rappaport (1998) also stresses the creation of commonality. Implementing the L.E.K. Consulting shareholder value approach provides organisations with a rigorous and consistent analysis framework while everybody shares a common framework for analysis, a common goal and a common language.

McKinsey & Co (Copeland et al., 2000) is noticeably of one mind, since it also stresses the alignment of business unit managers and employees with the priorities defined at corporate level. The process of defining value drivers is mentioned as one of the greatest boosters of this alignment. Likewise, PricewaterhouseCoopers (Read, 1997) refers to this positive influence on the creation of alignment in the company. Read refers to the importance of thoroughly explaining the principles of maximising shareholder value throughout the organisation. This process gives middle managers the opportunity to make front line managers aware of corporate strategy and implementation.

Armour and Mankins (2001), of Marakon Associates, emphasise the need for a specific mindset, based on financial performance combined with clear decision-making guidelines. The latter is thought to be the best sign that companies are developing a 'managing for value' culture. HOLT Value Associates (Madden, 1999) sees its CFROI model as an instrument to create a common language in the communication about performance and valuation. But it is also convinced that the empirical feedback, provided by the model, constitutes the perfect basis for continuous improvement.

Performance management and target setting

Performance management

Performance management and target setting transpire to be an important element in the value-based management process. The approaches of the six consultants concerning this topic are not unequivocal, but neither do they genuinely differ in our judgement. McTaggart *et al.* (1994) subdivide the performance management process into three activities: target setting, monitoring performance, and responding to differences between budgeted and real results. They emphasise that, in order to maximise shareholder value, two principles of performance management should be fulfilled. First, it is essential to work with plan-driven targets. This means that top management only defines the overall strategic and financial goals and then asks the business units to achieve them. The second principle concerns the creation of process integrity, which means that performance contracts are crafted and honoured by both the chief executive and business unit. Marakon Associates takes into account that every business unit should be unique when determining appropriate targets. Then again, the Marakon publicists remark that the financial measures for those targets should be set and monitored at general level.

For L.E.K. Consulting, performance management is built around the idea of developing an organisation-wide 'owner-oriented culture'. Kenney (Vol. II), vice president in L.E.K.'s Chicago office, mentions a three step process to create this 'owner-oriented culture' in a successful manner. Since he is convinced that companies need to adopt a performance measurement approach based on economic value measures, it is not surprising that the first step concentrates on 'overcoming the earning myopia'. Instead of evaluating revenue and earning growth measures, Kenney and his colleagues at L.E.K. Consulting recommend companies to consider measures of economic improvement. The second step, 'measure and reward long-term performance', is established to avoid dysfunctional behaviour of managers regarding the interests of shareholders. In Kenney's opinion, the creation of an ownership culture can only be successful when management is exposed to the long-term risks and rewards of ownership, which immediately explains the third and final step, 'convey risks and rewards of ownership'. As stated above, the ultimate goal of creating shareholder return is too aggregated to use at lower organisational levels. Rappaport (1998) therefore appeals to the performance measurement hierarchy, where he distinguishes total shareholder return as the preferred measure at corporate level. At operating unit level, he refers to SVA and leading indicators for the corresponding operating level. And last but not least, the specific key value drivers are defined as the most appropriate measures at the lower organisational levels. To facilitate the identification of the most accurate value drivers, Schor (Vol. I) describes a three-step process. The development of the value driver map of the corresponding business thereby forms the first step, while the value driver sensitivities are tested in the second step. The third and last step concerns the test for controllability.

The performance management system advised by McKinsey & Co (Copeland *et al.*, 2000) also consists of three elements. The first building block relates to the availability of a clearly defined value-creating strategy for business units, while the importance of alignment between the targets and the specific value drivers at business unit level comprises the second component. The structured performance reviews, during which the results are discussed in relation to the KPIs, are the third factor. These KPIs or operating value drivers are, as mentioned above, useful at the generic, business unit and front line level. McKinsey's spokespersons additionally refer to comparable key principles like those of Marakon Associates. The first principle of McKinsey & Co states that performance measurement needs to be tailor-made for the corresponding level. The second principle refers to combination of short-term and long-term targets, while the third one mentions the necessity of combining operational and financial performance measures. With regard to the fourth principle, Copeland *et al.* advise organisations to look for leading performance indicators. Clear objectives moreover, are supposed to have a motivational impact to achieve them and save time and effort for managers. Copeland *et al.* refer here to the ideal situation, where tailor-made scorecards are cascaded down in each business and every manager monitors the key value drivers that are important to them.

Target-setting (Black *et al.*, 1998) is mentioned as the first element in the performance management process of PricewaterhouseCoopers, since they stress the importance of determining those targets, based on share prices goals, after the explanation of the corporate analysis. The next step consists of linking those goals with the value drivers at the lower levels, where they argue that relevant value-focused measures are indispensable. To solve the problem of seeing the relation between the seven value drivers and the day-to day business of the company, Pricewaterhouse-Coopers suggests using micro drivers and thereby refer to the vision of Copeland. The seven value drivers mentioned by PricewaterhouseCoopers are the same as those of Rappaport, notwithstanding the fact that PricewaterhouseCoopers defines one of the value drivers, that is, value growth duration, as the competitive advantage period. After all, both value drivers are defined as the period of time a company has a positive net present value when discounted at the WACC. Economic business modelling can be very helpful in this process. Finally, they stress understanding and agreement on the value chain as a vital element.

Stern Stewart & Co (G. B. Stewart, 1999) refers, just like McKinsey & Co and PricewaterhouseCoopers, to the shareholder value network of Rappaport. Increasing EVA®, internalised through cross-functional teams, nevertheless remains the paramount objective in the performance management system of Stern Stewart & Co. G. B. Stewart detects six essential factors that influence the intrinsic value of the unit of analysis, also defined as EVA® drivers. This value driver model is not only applicable at corporate level, but also at business unit level and it can even be used for acquisition candidates. Management can, by means of policies and performance, influence four of these factors. The other two essential factors can only be affected by the market. The practical limitations of this value driver model – that is, the assumption of steady growth and steady returns from normalised values – explain why this model is only used to communicate the fundamentals of valuation in the organisation. Stern Stewart & Co therefore advises making use of the free cash flow model and the EVA® valuation approach instead of the value driver model.

Madden (1999) opposes the idea of a scorecard based on accounting and non-accounting variables. He tends to focus more on the learning process of internal performance measurement, due to the complex issues of the firm's internal performance measurement.

Target setting

Companies implementing value-based management counselled by Stern Stewart & Co (Ehrbar, 1998) are recommended to use EVA® goals in their target setting process. These EVA® goals are considered an excellent way of determining stretch targets, in which the EVA® driver analysis is seen as the instrument to evaluate the proposed plans for achieving those goals. The partners of Marakon Associates (McTaggart *et al.*, 1994; McTaggart and Gilllis, 1998; Kissel, Vol. IV; Kontes, Vol. IV) are convinced of the added value of plan-driven target setting. Overloading business units with targets does not fit with their vision. Kissel recognises that determining a single all-embracing performance standard combined with tailored goals and targets ought to be the best guarantee for successful target setting. Allowing business units to detect the most appropriate strategic alternatives in line with the proposed targets of economic growth is viewed as the most effective way to select the strategies that maximise economic profit over time.

In contrast with Marakon Associates and Stern Stewart & Co, McKinsey & Co advocates (Copeland *et al.*, 2000) an iterative target setting process. The McKinsey professionals view negotiation between the various organisational levels as a valuable instrument for managers to gain expertise about internal processes. This process also has an alleged constructive influence on the creation of internal commitment to achieve those targets.

Shareholder value maximisation not only forms the basis of the overall PricewaterhouseCoopers performance management process (Black *et al.*, 1998), it subsequently also plays a leading role in its target setting process. Black *et al.* state that these targets should be based on share price goals. Global targets need to be translated into targets at the lower organisational levels, more specifically the operational levels. The idea of translating the goals at higher levels, to more local targets is also supported by HOLT Value Associates and L.E.K. Consulting (Madden, 1999; Kenney, Vol. IX). Where HOLT Value Associates starts from the CFROI goals, shareholder return is the intermediate point in the approach of L.E.K. Consulting. Since generating shareholder return is synonymous with exceeding market expectations in the approach of the latter, it is vital for management to incorporate those expectations in the target setting process (Rappaport, 1998). At the lower organisational levels, that is, the operating level and the front line level, the performance measurement hierarchy forms the point of departure. The targets are set against the value drivers of the various levels and businesses, without overlooking the relevant expectations of the market on those corresponding organisational levels. Rappaport (1998) enumerates four sources of information to develop these 'market' expectations at business unit level: the business unit's operating plan; the unit's historical performance; competitive performance of value drivers; and market expectations for the whole company.

Reward system

It is not unexpected that all of the six mentioned VBM implementers give extensive attention to the rewarding issue, since the importance of the rewarding system on the behaviour of people is largely accepted. Our analysis and comparison of the different approaches is subdivided into three paragraphs: the first concentrates on the comparison of the different visions on the basis for rewarding, whereas the second focuses on the analysis of some general elements in the proposed compensation plan. The third and last paragraph deals with the key elements in each of their methodologies.

Basis for rewarding

Notwithstanding the fact that the basis for rewarding is viewed as a fundamental issue in the remuneration policy, there are some material differences between the various consultants. Stern Stewart & Co (Ehrbar, 1998; G. B. Stewart, 1999), Marakon Associates (McTaggart *et al.*, 1994; Armour and Mankins, 2001) and PricewaterhouseCoopers (Black *et al.*, 1998) subscribe the idea of linking rewarding with realised value creation. This is in contrast with McKinsey & Co, where the rewarding is based on the number of executed value creation activities. Madden (1999) suggests linking compensation not to the extent of realised value creation, but on an empirical comparison. The idea of the L.E.K. Consulting advisors to reward incentives on superior performance, defined as performance that equals or excels the performance of the company's peer group or market indices, bears more resemblance to the rewarding policies of HOLT Value Associates, than to the other financial planning providers (Rappaport, 1999; Kenney, Vol. II).

General elements of the compensation scheme

Stern Stewart & Co (G. B. Stewart, 1999) is convinced of the idea of making managers into owners by means of a specific rewarding system. This viewpoint immediately explains why Stern Stewart & Co keeps harping on about the idea that the company's plans should be designed in such a way that they expose executives and shareholders to the same risk (Stern *et al.*, 2001). The rewarding system proposed by Stern Stewart & Co starts with rewarding top management and is gradually extended towards the organisational levels. Despite the statement that EVA® incentives work at all levels (Stern *et al.*, 2001) on condition that the evaluation and rewarding is based exclusively on factors that can be influenced, the use of this incentive scheme at shop floor level is rather exceptional. Union resistance and inability to understand the link between the proposed EVA® incentives and day-to-day performance are the most cited reasons to exclude blue-collar workers from bonuses based on EVA®. Even G. B. Stewart suggests limiting the rewarding component of the EVA® Financial Management System to the management level, certainly in the first phases of its implementation. Marakon Associates (McTaggart *et al.*, 1994) agrees with Stern Stewart & Co and more in particular with the opinion of G. B. Stewart, since Marakon also focuses on rewarding top management. Top management is here defined as the chief executive, the general managers of the business units and the most important shared resources units together with all those reporting directly to them. McTaggart views the alignment between top management and the governing objective as vital to support the further internal changes.

In spite of the fact that both consulting firms support the idea of deploying the rewarding policy throughout the organisation, it appears they suggest concentrating on top levels first. This idea is in contrast with the perception of McKinsey & Co (Copeland *et al.*, 2000) and PricewaterhouseCoopers (Black *et al.*, 1998), since these consulting firms advocate that rewarding systems should be fully implemented in the organisation. The consultants of HOLT Value Associates are more prudent and (Madden, 1999) adhere to the idea of David Walker, the vice-president of finance at Procter & Gamble, who suggests waiting some time before linking the reward system to the outcome of the CFROI model. Walker is convinced that it is advisable to gain some experience with the CFROI model before evaluating and rewarding people based on those results. Rappaport (1998) shares in a certain way the opinion of Madden with regard to the introduction of new performance and incentive systems with the overall implementation of value-based management. Since Rappaport is aware of the fact that a premature introduction of performance measures can seriously compromise the entire shareholder value programme, he suggests waiting with this link until management fully understands and accepts the measures that it is held accountable for. Smith, one of the partners in L.E.K.'s London office, specifies their vision by explaining how valuable it is to gradually introduce these value-based incentives (Smith, Vol. XIV). He is a strong advocate of starting with incentives that only track the most important performance indicators, since this will provide encouragement to achieve the collective goals in the overall mix of compensation.

On the other hand, there are more similarities with the viewpoint of Stern Stewart & Co and Marakon Associates than with the opinion of HOLT Value Associates. The partners of L.E.K. Consulting, just like Stern Stewart & Co, underline the importance of putting executives at the same risks as shareholders. Kenney (Vol. II) draws attention to this when he lists the steps to create an 'ownership-oriented culture'. Another parallel between Stern Stewart & Co, Marakon Associates and L.E.K. Consulting is situated at the rewarding level. The advisers of Stern Stewart & Co and L.E.K. Consulting, both want to extend the reward system to all organisational levels, based on one overall performance goal; EVA® in the approach of Stern Stewart & Co and shareholder return in the shareholder value approach of L.E.K. Consulting. And although both are convinced that their suggested evaluation measure is applicable at all organisational levels, they are aware that these measures can be viewed as too aggregate. Therefore, both suggest translating these measures into controllable value drivers at the corresponding levels.

Key elements in the rewarding policy

As mentioned above, each of the consulting firms, with the exception of HOLT Value Associates, has developed a complete rewarding methodology, each with its own distinguishing features. Stern Stewart & Co is renowned for its bonus bank concept (Stern Stewart, 1999; Stern *et al.*, 2001; Young and O'Byrne, 2001). Stern Stewart & Co considers its system the best alternative for putting managers at the same risk as the company owners. One of the most important advantages of this system lies in the fact that the horizons of managers are stretched from short-term to longer term, since the exceptional part of the remuneration is banked forward, while the other, normal, component is paid out. Part of this exceptional bonus will then be distributed in the following years, depending on the results. There are two popular versions of the bonus bank, the 'threshold' and the 'all-in'. The bonus bank idea is characterised by uncapped or unlimited bonuses, in either a positive or negative manner, and the EVA® targets are determined by a formula instead of negotiations. It is important to be aware of the fact that negative bonuses are possible in this system. Despite the fact that the bonuses of everyone in the organisation are best tied to improvements in EVA® (G. B. Stewart, 1999; Stern *et al.*, 2001; Young and O'Byrne, 2001), the EVA® plan is preferably based on the results of the corresponding organisational level. This implies that the evaluation of top-level executives is based on the performance of the entire company, where the rewarding of managers is related to the performance of the corresponding unit or division. To encourage co-operation between various divisions, Stern Stewart & Co suggests splitting the compensation of chief divisional executives. Part of their compensation is then based on the corporate results, while the other part is based on the divisional results. Stern *et al.* emphasise that specific 'value drivers', like capital and equipment efficiency, are best incorporated when the EVA® plan is extended to the shop floor level. Stern Stewart & Co advises extending the rewarding of top management with an additional incentive plan, based on leveraged stock options. It appears that the rewarding policy of Stern Stewart & Co is exclusively based on financial determinants, but this is not true. Despite its emphasis on cash rewarding and other financial incentives, G. B. Stewart (1999) recognises the impact of internal rewarding and subscribes to the idea that the feeling of 'ownership' is primarily a matter of attitude. Pride, sensible risk-taking and accepting responsibility are necessary conditions to make managers into owners.

The impact of strategy is not only vital in the performance management process of Marakon Associates (McTaggart *et al.*, 1994), but also plays a significant role in its rewarding methodology. Marakon Associates states that financial rewards need to be the result of the development of the most appropriate strategies. McTaggart *et al.* refer to the performance management process in which business unit managers sign a (perform-ance) contract with the chief executive and engage themselves to fulfil the agreements. As mentioned above, this is, according to Marakon Associ-ates, the best guarantee to align the business unit strategies with the corporate governing objective of maximising shareholder value. This illus-trates the suggestion of McTaggart *et al.* to use the performance contracts as the basis for the evaluation of general and business unit managers. The consultants of Marakon Associates share the opinion of Stern Stewart & Co in relation to the rewarding basis. Marakon Associates advises using corporate results as a point of reference for the compensation of top management. Compensation is preferably based on the performance of some internal financial indicators, applied to all organisational levels, combined with the results of the company's total shareholder returns, in comparison with similar companies. The financial and strategic targets on business unit level, resulting from the strategy development process, should be employed for evaluating business unit level performance.

'Relative pay for relative performance' is the credo of Marakon Associ-ates. This implies that the compensation depends on their own perform-ance compared with the results in similar companies. Another similarity in the approaches of Stern Stewart & Co (Stern *et al.*, 2001) and Marakon Associates (McTaggart *et al.*, 1994) lies in the fact that both suggest using single-year or single period-by-period performance measures for the compensation. However, the two consultants do not share the same idea about the payout policy. The partners of Marakon Associates are not convinced of the advantages of the bonus bank system, since they prefer to disburse the complete bonus in cash. They state that the un-certainty about future bonuses should be limited to whether the targets will be achieved in the coming years. They consider stock options as a good alternative, but only in small or start-up companies. They further-more subscribe to the idea, just like Stern Stewart & Co, that companies should support their managers to choose stock instead of cash.

McKinsey & Co (Koller, 1994; Copeland *et al.*, 2000) stresses the idea of linking the behaviour and performance of individuals with value creating activities and rewarding. One of the most important elements in this approach is the establishment of challenging targets, which implies that the proposed targets are higher than the median in comparable com-panies. Thus far, McKinsey can be considered to be on the same wave-length as Marakon. A distinguishing feature in its approach is the emphasis on the importance of differentiation in rewarding. It is convinced that, in particular for high-performing executives, the differentiation in rewarding is much more important than the total pay. This idea is closely linked with their emphasis on the advantages of visualising the realised performance.

The approach of McKinsey & Co also shows, despite the differences, more general similarities with the approaches of the previously described consultants. The partners of McKinsey & Co also subscribe the idea of linking the rewards with the performance of the corresponding organisational levels. They suggest linking the evaluation of individuals to the controllable KPIs for which they are responsible, in order to guarantee alignment between the targets on business unit level and the actions of individuals. The return to shareholders and economic profit are mentioned as appropriate measures for the evaluation of the CEO and the corporate staff. Business managers can be evaluated on the economic profit metric and the EBIT-Capital utilisation. The latter metric, combined with individual operating value drivers, is suitable for the performance evaluation of functional managers. These individual operating value drivers are, furthermore, appropriate for the evaluation of the corporate staff and all other employees. McKinsey & Co thereby mentions the requirement of frequent performance reviews. Another resemblance between the previously mentioned consultants is the idea that short-term targets are best linked with long-term ones. McKinsey & Co (Koller, 1994) and Stern Stewart & Co share moreover a comparable vision on the necessary elements in the reward package, since they are also convinced that monetary rewarding is only one means of motivating people. They recognise the importance of financial incentives and even express their aversion to bonus caps, but advise companies to combine these financial incentives with career opportunities and the creation of a culture based on values and beliefs where people feel satisfied about their way of working.

The rewarding methodology of PricewaterhouseCoopers (Black *et al.*, 1998) shows many similarities with the previously described methodologies. The partners of Marakon Associates have already mentioned the importance of strategy in the rewarding system and these again turn up in the rewarding policy of PricewaterhouseCoopers. They stress the fact that the compensation system needs to be in line with the strategy. They share with Stern Stewart & Co the idea of long-term incentive plans. Economic performance, creating the groundwork for rewarding as mentioned in the approach of Stern Stewart & Co and Marakon Associates is here once more valid. Since PricewaterhouseCoopers believes, as do the three other consulting firms, that no one measure is suitable for all hierarchical levels, it suggests using different performance measures for different levels. These measures need to be controllable on the corresponding level and a combination of key macro and operating value drivers is preferred. One of the distinguishing characteristics in the approach of PricewaterhouseCoopers is the use of time frames with different lengths for different hierarchical levels, which means that incentives on a higher level are coupled to performance over a longer period of time.

Since exceeding the threshold standard for superior performance forms the basis of the VBM system of L.E.K. Consulting, it is not surprising that the SVA measure is determined as the benchmark in their reward system (Rhoads, Vol. X). Before dealing with the distinguishing features of L.E.K's rewarding methodology, we first deal with the analogies *vis-à-vis* the previously described methodologies. Several partners of this consulting firm explicitly agree about the importance of consistency between short-term and long-term performance measures. The rewarding basis hierarchy consists of two aspects: the performance measurement hierarchy and the determination of most appropriate goals on the corresponding echelons. Total shareholder return, suggested at corporate level, is translated to SVA and other leading indicators of value for the operating managers. These measures are in turn translated to specific key value drivers at the lowest organisational levels (Rappaport, 1998; 1999; Rhoads, Vol. X). To determine threshold standards on the various levels, Rappaport (1987; 1998) suggests using the market expectations analysis, an approach that completely fits with his 'pay for performance' vision (Rappaport, 1999). The goals for the CEO and the corporate level executives will be based on exceeding a peer or the market index. The operating unit managers have the task of exceeding the market expectations. Last, but not least, the goals of operating unit employees will be based on the achievement of key value driver results (Rappaport, 1998; 1999; Rhoads, Vol. X).

Kenney and the other advisors of L.E.K. Consulting (Kenney, Vol. II; Rappaport and Mauboussin, Vol. XVIII; Rappaport, 1998; 1999; Rhoads, Vol. X) clearly support the rewarding policy developed by Stern Stewart & Co as the bonus bank. First of all, they defend the idea that incentives should be matched with the levers that can be influenced by the individual. Furthermore, they agree on a rolling year performance period of three to five years and do not have any objections regarding the non-existence of caps or maximum (minimum) bonuses. Similar to the New York-based financial planning advisor, L.E.K. Consulting argues that a three to five-year performance period counters the problem of dysfunctional behaviour, certainly in bad years and thus is a much more accurate solution than reducing the threshold performance targets in such years (Rappaport, 1998). Notwithstanding the fact of its awareness of the limitations of rewarding people with stock options for the operating executives and the other employees deeper down in the organisation, it does stress that stock options are very suitable as a performance measure for the highest organisational level (Rappaport, 1998).

The major distinction in the approach of the L.E.K. Consulting advisers lies in their ideas about employee remuneration based on indexed options (Rappaport and Mauboussin, Vol. XVIII) (Roath, Vol. IV). In this way, they want to avoid paying for suboptimal performance. An indexed option is based on the premise that the strike price of the option is indexed to a peer group average, also defined as the average of their competitors, or a market index. In the end, the choice between those two is much less important than the switch to establish such an index (Rappaport, 1998; 1999). Various partners of L.E.K. Consulting mention advantages like being a fair measure and aligning the interests of managers with those of the shareholders (Rappaport, 1999; Rhoads, Vol. X). They know, however, that it will be difficult to get these ideas accepted within the company and therefore recommend that the indexed options packages should be structured so that exceptional performers can earn greater returns than they could with conventional options. Therefore, two stimuli are best incorporated into the packages. Companies should first augment the number of options they grant to executives. And second, Rappaport advises working with discounted indexed options, which are options characterised by a lower exercise price (Rappaport, 1999).

Training and education

Extensive research on the key elements in the value-based management approach has revealed that changes in the mindset of the individuals and in the mindset and culture of the entire company are manifest and probably necessary for a successful VBM implementation. It is therefore not surprising that all consulting firms, with the exception of HOLT Value Associates, have developed their own training and education programme to support the implementation and adoption of value-based management thinking.

The professionals of Stern Stewart & Co (Stern *et al.*, 2001; Young and O'Byrne, 2001) are aware of the need to change the mindset of everyone in the organisation. They make a clear distinction between the formal training, at the beginning of the VBM process, and the continuous communication after the implementation of the EVA® framework. The top-down training, in which all employees at any organisational level learn the basics of EVA®, is typical. Stern *et al.* mention two training approaches. EVA® becomes part of the strategic overhaul of the entire company in the first approach, whereas there is no strategic refocusing in the second approach. They furthermore stress that companies should continue the communication about EVA with the entire workforce after the training phase.

The partners of Marakon Associates (Kissel, Vol. IV; McTaggart *et al.*, 1994) are on the same wavelength as the people of Stern Stewart & Co. Kissel is convinced that top management needs to take responsibility for continuous reinforcement of VBM ideas through their communication and decisions. The similarity with the idea of Stern Stewart & Co is clear, both choose top-down communication and both stress the impor-tance of continuous communication. The focus in the content of their communication differs however. While Stern Stewart & Co tries to explain the EVA® concept throughout the organisation, McTaggart *et al.* are more concerned about making everybody aware of the governing objective. Business unit managers need to understand that they have to concentrate on those strategies that maximise the governing objective.

Not only Marakon Associates and Stern Stewart & Co, but also the professionals of L.E.K. Consulting acknowledge the importance of reinforcing VBM ideas through education and training. Both Rappaport and Smith stress the importance of continuous communication (Rappaport, Vol. V; Smith, Vol. XIV). Rappaport states that shareholder value is typically implemented in three broad phases. The first phase focuses on senior management, since it is first of all important that senior management is convinced of a genuine need for change. When senior management is won over, the appropriate details of change must be defined and properly introduced in the second phase. Subsequently, in the third phase, it is important to reinforce change to ensure that it is sustained. Smith also emphasises the need for persistent communication at all organisational levels. In this respect, he suggests tailor-made educa-tion and value enhancement workshops, because these are seen as helpful tools to demonstrate how the daily decisions of every individual, indepen-dent of the organisational level, influence shareholder value. Education occupies a prominent position in the shareholder value approach of this adviser in financial planning since they developed a shareholder value education agenda (Rappaport, 1998). Without claiming that this agenda will meet the needs of every organisation, they are however convinced that some of the topics are unbearable in almost all programmes. Another distinguishing feature is the 'train the trainers' approach. According to them, this approach is not only the perfect answer for the shortage of teaching resources, but also guarantees a broader acceptance of 'owner-ship' for the ideas of shareholder value.

McKinsey & Co (Copeland *et al.*, 2000; Koller, 1994) suggests starting with a survey, since it thinks of the difficulties of immediately focusing on changing beliefs and values. A survey can help to get an idea of the beliefs of people, and the results form the perfect basis to start a discussion and all work together on the creation of a new mindset. Despite its different way of working, it also wants to reach the entire organisation. In its opinion, communication is best focused on value-creating issues.

The PricewaterhouseCoopers training and communication plan (Read, 1997; Black *et al.*, 1998) does not differ much from the plans of Stern Stewart & Co and Marakon Associates. All three share the preference for top-down communication. PricewaterhouseCoopers here sees an important role for the CEO and the CFO and is aware of the impact of endorsement from top management. Another element in its plan is the education of the entire workforce with regard to the shareholder value theme. Black *et al.* believe that the introduction of shareholder value programmes, which are built around the share price goal, simplifies communication and has a positive influence on motivation.

Facilitators for the implementation

A well-founded training and education plan will not be sufficient for a successful implementation of value-based management. All the consultants therefore recommend facilitators that support the implementation process. The establishment of a formal implementation team (Stern *et al.*, 2001; Young and O'Byrne, 2001) is one of the recommendations of Stern Stewart & Co. The team consists of representatives from finance and accounting and planning and operations and their role is to report their findings to the steering committee. The firm's executive or the management committee, together with senior management, the CFO, the CEO and the head of the human resources department, forms this committee. These people are charged with the most important policy decisions and the design and structure of EVA®. Besides their role in the steering committee, the CFO and CEO have another important task – communicating their commitment to the EVA® framework within the company. The implementation team is, in addition, recommended to keep in touch with the consultants to ensure the transfer of knowledge and to anticipate problems.

The partners of Marakon Associates (McTaggart *et al.*, 1994; Armour and Mankins, 2001) also assign an important role to the CEO and top management. They are seen as the champions to drive the implementation and are the best guarantee for the establishment and the sustainability of value creation as a core competence. They expect the chief executive to be the visible leader of the VBM process. Since this needs to be the CEO's highest priority, he or she is expected to be totally committed to a successful implementation and well informed about all the VBM principles.

McKinsey & Co (Koller, 1994; Copeland *et al.*, 2000) shares the idea of Marakon Associates about the important role of the CEO and top management as catalysts in a value-based management company. Nevertheless, it thinks the support of top management will not be sufficient. It therefore recommends an extensive participation of the business unit managers in the value driver analysis, since this will not only increase the insight of those managers in their value-based thinking but also influence their feeling of ownership.

Black *et al.* (1998) mention the need of sponsorship by the CEO. But again this will not be enough and they therefore advise that senior management and the board of directors contribute to the sponsorship commission of the CEO. The consultants of PricewaterhouseCoopers furthermore recommends the development of a value transformation programme where a value transformation team, consisting of representatives of the major departments, will have a positive influence on the internal ownership and the internal communication regarding the shareholder value approach. This team can then be involved in the education of every hierarchical level in relation to measuring and managing economic value.

According to various partners of L.E.K. Consulting, senior commitment is defined as the single most important factor to implement the shareholder value approach successfully throughout the company. The CEO, the board and management need to be convinced of the usefulness of implementing the shareholder value approach before the implementation has any chance of succeeding (Rappaport, 1998; Roath, Vol. IV; Smith, Vol. XIV). Even though L.E.K. Consulting does not explicitly stress the importance of establishing an implementation team, they are nonetheless aware of several facilitating elements. The timing of the implementation, the suggestion to begin with a committed CFO and the advice to tailor for operating managers are only a couple of the facilitators referred to that increase the commitment of top management and thus indirectly contribute in the company-wide development of the shareholder value approach.

Another important issue is the trade-off between a full-scale implementation or the implementation on a less broader scale. The extent of diversification and centralisation together with the degree of commitment of the CEO are potential determining factors. It is strongly recommended to follow an evolutionary path in highly decentralised companies, active in several industries where the CEO is not totally committed (Rappaport, 1998).

Benchmarking

The issue of benchmarking is closely related to value-based metrics. Stern Stewart & Co (Ehrbar, 1998) proposes EVA® as a basis for benchmarking. The accuracy of the market value can be tested by comparing the market value of the company with the sum of the EVA®s of the different plans. Not only corporate performance, but also internal performance can be measured with EVA®. After EVA® is disaggregated with the use of EVA drivers, it is easy to detect which business units, product lines, etc., are satisfactory and which are not.

In the opinion of Marakon Associates (McTaggart *et al.*, 1994), benchmarking at corporate level is best based on the comparison of key management processes like strategic planning, resource allocation and so on. This exercise might reveal some competitive advantages. Besides the comparison based on the key performance processes, more and more companies compare their corporate results with market averages and with peer companies. Benchmarking at the business unit level is best based on the identification and comparison of strategic value drivers.

McKinsey & Co (Koller, 1994) recommends DCF, together with economic profit for benchmarking activities at business unit level. Since this consulting firm states that DCF is the best metric to evaluate the performance of a company, it is not surprising that this is also mentioned as the best metric for the corporate level. Copeland *et al.* (2000) indicate here that economic profit and market value do not measure the same thing. The first one measures the realised value creation while the second measures short-term and long-term future value creation expectations.

To understand the ideas of PricewaterhouseCoopers (Read, 1997; Black *et al.*, 1998) about benchmarking, it is important to take into account that they define benchmarking in a broader manner, since they extend the interpretation of competitors. Regarding the emphasis of Read on the significance of cash flow performance, it is not surprising that this consulting firm suggests corporate benchmarking based on cash flow performance with companies competing for the same investment funds. The performance of the company can also be analysed by the seven value drivers; these, defined at business unit level, are also the ideal instruments to review the performance at that organisational level. According to HOLT Value Associates (Madden, 1999), the CFROI model can be used to compare the current performance with the historical results or to compare the company's own performance with other, domestic and foreign companies.

The partners of L.E.K. Consulting combine some of the ideas of the previously mentioned consultants (Rhoads, Vol. X; Rappaport, 1998; Smith, Vol. XIV). Rhoads defines relative total shareholder return or the comparison of the company's total return with a group of peer leaders as the single best measure. The preference for this measure is based on the fact that it is free from accounting distortions and that it is not biased by market expectations or industry specific price movements. Since DCF is after all the basis for shareholder thinking and since valuations derived from DCF take into account all of the characteristics from the true market value, it is not surprising that DCF is referred to as the best proxy in the absence of a true current benchmark (Smith, Vol. XIV). DCF is then not only applicable for benchmarking at corporate level, but it can also be used at lower organisational levels. The sources of information for target-setting at lower organisational levels, as specified by Rappaport, can probably reveal very constructive information for benchmarking at these levels (Rappaport, 1998).

5. CONCLUSION

Value-based management can be defined as an integrated management control system that measures, encourages and supports the creation of net worth. It appears that value creation and the maximisation of shareholder wealth is a very fashionable topic these days, both in practice as well as in the academic field. A number of conceptual reasons indicate that increasing shareholder value does not conflict with the long-term interests of other stakeholders. On the contrary, value-based management systems are specifically acknowledged to reduce lack of goal congruence between the owners of the firm and its constituents. Moreover, as an integrated management approach, VBM is said to tackle most of the perceived inefficiencies of traditional management accounting measures and systems.

We have argued that shareholder focus and stakeholder theory could be reconciled. Despite the fact that the objectives of the shareholder and the other stakeholder groups do not always converge, it is recognised that working together to realise the mission of the firm is the most efficient way to achieve some of their own objectives. Furthermore, the maximisation of shareholder value does not have to conflict with the stakeholder approach if the value-based management process within the organisation is combined with socially responsible behaviour.

The essence of value maximisation is to invest in projects that will produce a rate of return that is higher than the cost of capital. A value-based management system induces managers to maximise the economic worth of an organisation by allocating its assets to their best use. Capital is not for free; a certain cost must be calculated-in to use it. The reason for this is scarcity. If a company gets the opportunity to invest capital, another company is denied the chance to use it. Earning the cost of capital is not just a financial matter, it is merely the market mandate. On account of the residual income theory, VBM gives organisations a yardstick to distinguish good growth from bad growth.

We divided the value-based performance measures into two segments. If the value or the marginal change in the value of an organisation can be measured by using the information on the stock market, we attribute the metric to the listed perspective. If the warranted value of the company is estimated indirectly using an alternative valuation model, we qualify the metric as pertaining to the not-listed perspective. We discussed a non-exhaustive collection of measures. It depends on the use and the specific business case whether residual income-type measures are preferred over discounted cash flow approaches or any other method of quantification. The same holds for single-period measures versus multi-period measures.

In the listed perspective we find total shareholder return and market value added. In order to determine both measures we rely on information from the capital markets. Total shareholder return is an appraisal of value creation or destruction based on incorporation of the overall rate of return of the investment without evaluating whether or not this return exceeds the cost of equity. Market value added is a cumulative formula that represents corporate performance. Apart from theoretical considerations, empirical research has revealed that MVA would be a more effective investment tool than other measures.

Evaluating not only the net worth of a company but also the value of business units and different product-market combinations requires metrics that do not necessarily call for stock market data. The not-listed perspective encompasses economic value added, equity spread approach, cash flow return on investment and shareholder value added.

EVA® and its look-alikes are residual income-type metrics, which are being used by value-based management practitioners as measures of the excess value created by firms and managers. Economic value added is by far the highest ranking metric in the popularity polls. EVA® is regarded as a fairly simple but powerful yardstick both due to its hypothetical correspondence with market value added and due to its straightforward management objectives. Nevertheless, its popularity should not conceal its shortcomings; for example, the fact it ignores inflation or is based on erroneous time periods, its ambiguous empirical relation with MVA and so on.

The equity-spread approach is a return-based single-period measure that uses the same variables as the market to book ratio, which is a well known and broadly accepted yardstick among the financial community. Both Marakon Associates and HOLT Value Associates apply this Gordon model-based approach in their value-based management practice.

From a multi-period perspective we have selected two discounted cash flow-based measures: cash flow return on investment (CFROI) and shareholder value added (SVA). CFROI is said to be very useful for valuation by both managers and security analysts working for corporations. While it is a noteworthy metric from a conceptual point of view, CFROI is often depicted as a complex financial measure device. When cash flow return on investment that gauges the internal rate of return of an entire company is compared with its real cost of capital and then multiplied by the capital employed, we calculate a residual income that Boston Consulting Group has branded 'cash value added'. 'Shareholder value added' was first described by Alfred Rappaport who established a tremendous managerial step forward in the field of value-based management by breaking SVA down into a comprehensive model of seven key drivers of shareholder value.

From a conceptual point of view, we agree with Copeland *et al.* when they state that there is no perfect performance measure. Furthermore, our review indicates that value-based management only by means of alignment and coherence of the organisation's limited resources becomes a holistic, strategy-oriented management technique that can produce a remarkable performance breakthrough. This chapter concentrates on six consulting firms which developed frameworks claiming to bring value-based management to life: Stern Stewart & Co; Marakon Associates; McKinsey and Co; PricewaterhouseCoopers; L.E.K. Consulting; and HOLT Value Associates. Our comparison of the VBM systems from the selected consulting firms reveals some similarities between the approaches, but also demonstrates different accents and some clear distinctions.

With regard to management focus, all six consulting firms draw attention to the imperative of maximising shareholder value as the principal performance objective. The same unanimity exists about the conviction that the interests of all stakeholder groups are best served when putting the shareholder first. There appears to be less consensus *vis-à-vis* the fundamentals for value creation; Marakon, Stern Stewart, L.E.K. and HOLT primarily refer to strategy while McKinsey mentions metrics as a cornerstone of the framework and PricewaterhouseCoopers above all concentrates on organisational design.

Apart from Stern Stewart, L.E.K. Consulting and HOLT, the main elements of the approaches of the consultants reveal similarities with the basic mechanisms of a management control system as defined by Anthony and Govindarajan (2001). Apart from their different emphases, all three elements (culture, structure, and systems) are elaborated by Marakon, McKinsey and PricewaterhouseCoopers. HOLT's VBM framework, on the other hand, is primarily a valuation system, L.E.K. Consulting builds its approach predominantly on culture and systems and Stern Stewart is basically oriented towards systems with a measurement programme combined with a management system, an incentive compensation plan and training. None of the consulting firms denies the importance or the impact of external communication, which is mainly focused on the investment community at large. The approach with regard to internal contribution is more manneristic and always has a pedagogic undertone.

Since almost all consultants embed value-based management in a strategic process, each of them refers to a more or less characteristic strategy development and deployment methodology. Marakon has a well endowed and distinguishing framework for strategy formulation. All others, except for HOLT which has the least articulated visioning process, refer to the well-known strategy gurus like Porter, Treacy and Wiersema and so on. Although the elements of the strategy deployment technique differ, all professional service firms except for HOLT refer to a value driver model that resembles Rappaport's driver tree scheme.

With articles like 'Metric Wars' in the more popular press, it should be clear that metrics are used to establish a competitive advantage. All consultants thereby seem to concurrently offer a single and a multi-period measure. Stern Stewart is certainly the most renowned in the VBM field for its EVA® and MVA system. Marakon promotes equity spread and economic profit. McKinsey also uses EP as a single period measure but refers to enterprise DCF in a multi-period interval. L.E.K. Consulting refers to the shareholder value network with SVA and marginal change in residual income. Cash flow return on investment positioned HOLT as a reference in the field. PricewaterhouseCoopers appears to embrace multiple measures but has a predisposition for CFROI, SVA and a tailored free cash flow model.

Investment decisions are inextricably bound up with the strategy development process. All consultants, except Marakon, refer to specific discounted cash flow models to guide managers in the investment decision and resource allocation process. Stern Stewart and HOLT appears to be very attached to its proprietary models while McKinsey and L.E.K. Consulting refer to more recent developments in the field as there are real option techniques, market signal analysis and so on. By setting out broad-spectrum boundaries and describing more general principles and policies without stipulating an explicit model, Marakon Associates approaches investment decisions from a different angle. Since mergers and acquisitions can be considered as a specific kind of investment decision, it is not surprising that the same holds for the M&A issue.

All professional services firms describe the impact of value-based management on collaboration. VBM is commonly regarded as an appropriate instrument to encourage everyone to work together and to align people's behaviour with the interests of shareholders.

One of the most important elements in a value-based management process transpires to be performance management and target setting. The approaches of the six consultants towards this theme are not unequivocal, but neither do they genuinely differ. Most striking is the clear focus on a single critical performance objective in casu maximisation of shareholder value. None of them actually prescribes a performance management model like the balanced scorecard does, but all consultants clearly depict essential elements and general principles. In order to give some guidance to managers, Stern Stewart, McKinsey, L.E.K. Consulting and PricewaterhouseCoopers refer to their proprietary adaptation of the Rappaport shareholder value network. Both Stern Stewart and HOLT stress the use of EVA® goals and CFROI goals in the company's target setting process.

Since a proper reward system links both performance management and internal collaboration, it should be no surprise that Stern Stewart, Marakon, McKinsey, L.E.K. Consulting and PricewaterhouseCoopers give extensive attention to the issue of remuneration. Only HOLT is rather reticent about linking its CFROI model to reward systems. All others, in one way or another, consider the remuneration scheme as a means of aligning management and the owners of the company. Stern Stewart more or less brands its EVA®-based system of stretched and uncapped rewards as the 'bonus bank'. The aversion to capped bonuses is also a distinguishing feature of McKinsey's and L.E.K's approach, but differs from the Stern Stewart model in the sense that performance targets are tailored to different levels and linked to controllable KPIs instead of being generically linked to EVA®. Marakon recommends benchmarking the company's performance to its peers and therefore deliberately directs its remuneration scheme to top management.

Although our review has revealed that the performance management systems of all VBM approaches are to some extent all-purpose and largely dependent on beliefs and principles, it should be clear that each consulting firm except HOLT draws attention to the prerequisite to have a specific mindset or culture in order to successfully implement value-based management. It is therefore not surprising that the other five developed their own training and education programme to support the adoption of value-based thinking. The content, however, differs substantially. While Stern Stewart mainly focuses on EVA®, Marakon, L.E.K.

Consulting and McKinsey built a training and education curriculum on strategy development and implementing strategies that ensure value creation.

Finally, a well-founded training and education plan is not considered to be the only critical factor in a successful value-based management implementation. Each consulting firm therefore recommends the visible sponsorship of the programme by top management and the installation of a formal implementation team.

REFERENCES

Anonymous, 'Finance can inhibit shareholder value creation', *Management Accounting*, April, 1998, 10–11.

Anthony, R., and Govindarajan, V., *Management Control Systems*, International Edition, 2001, McGraw-Hill Irwin, p. 778.

Armitage, H. M., and Fog, V., 'Economic value creation: What every management accountant should know', *CMA Magazine*, October, 1996, 21–4.

Armour, E., and Mankins, M. C., 'Back to the future', *Journal of Business Strategy*, July/August, 2001, 22–27.

Arnold, G. (1998) *Corporate Financial Management*, 1998, Pitman Publishing, p. 1050.

Bacidore, J. M., Boquist, J. A., Milbourn, T. T., and Thakor, A. V., 'The search for the best financial performance measure', *Financial Analysts Journal*, May/June, 1997, 11–20.

Bannister, R. J., and Jesuthasan, R., 'Is your company ready for value-based management?' *Journal of Business Strategy*, March/April, 1997, 12–15.

Biddle, G. C., Bowen, R. M., and Wallace, J. S., 'Does EVA® beat earnings? Evidence on associations with stock returns and firm values', *Journal of Accounting and Economics*, December, Vol. 24, No. 3, 1997, 301–336.

Black, A., Wright, P., and Bachman, J., *In Search of Shareholder Value*, 1998, Pitman Publishing, p. 292.

Boulos, F., Haspeslagh, P., and Noda, T., *Getting the Value out of Value-Based Management*, 2001, INSEAD survey, p. 54.

Brealey, R., and Myers, S. (2000) *Principles of corporate finance*, Sixth Edition, 2000, McGraw-Hill Irwin, p. 1092.

Brewer, P., Chandra, G., and Hock, C., 'Economic Value Added (EVA): Its uses and limitations', *SAM Advanced Management Journal*, Vol. 64, Issue 2, Spring, 1999, 4–11.

Bromwich, M., 'Value based financial management systems', *Management Accounting Research*, September, 1998, 387–9.

Bromwich, M., and Walker, M., 'Residual income past and future', *Management Accounting Research*, September, 1998, 391–419.

Brown, J., Macaskill, D., and Owen, H., 'The Stern Stewart and Marakon Shareholder Value Added Metrics: A comparative study with implications for the management accountant', Napier University Business School. Paper presented at the *BAA (Scotland) Conference* in September, 2000, 37 pp.

Christopher, M., and Ryals, L., 'Supply chain strategy: Its impact on shareholder value', *International Journal of Logistics Management*, Vol. 10, No. 1, 1999, 1–10.

Condon, J., and Goldstein, J., 'Value-Based Management – the only way to manage for value', *Accountancy Ireland*, October, 1998, 10–12.

Copeland, T. E., 'Why value value?', *McKinsey Quarterly*, No. 4, 1994, 97–109.

Copeland, T. E., Koller, T. M., and Murrin, J. (2000) *Valuation, Measuring and Managing the Value of Companies*, Third Edition, 2000, John Wiley & Sons, 550 pp.

Dechow, P. M., Hutton, A. P., and Sloan, R. G., 'An empirical assessment of the residual income valuation model', *Journal of Accounting & Economics*, January, 1999, 1–34.

Dodd, J. L., and Chen, S., 'EVA: A new panacea?', *Business and Economic Review*, July/September, 1996, Vol. 42, 26–28.

Donaldson, T., and Preston, L. E., 'The stakeholder theory of the corporation: Concepts, evidence, and implications', *Academy of Management Review*, Vol. 20, No. 1, 1995, 65–91.

Ehrbar, A., *EVA – the Real Key to Creating Wealth*, First Edition, 1998, John Wiley & Sons, 234 pp.

Eisenhardt, K., 'Agency theory: An assessment and review', *Academy of Management Review*, Vol. 14, 57–74, 1989.

Eiteman, D. K., Stonehill, A. I., and Moffett, M. H. (1999) *Multinational Business Finance*, Eighth Edition, 1999, Addison-Wesley, 854 pp.

England, J. D., 'Don't be afraid of phantom stock', *Compensation & Benefits Review*, September/October, 1992, 39–46.

Fama, E. F., 'Agency problems and the theory of the firm', *Journal of Political Economy*, Vol. 88, 1980, 288–307.

Fera, N., 'Using shareholder value to evaluate strategic choices', *Management Accounting*, November, 1997, 47–51.

Grant, R. M., *Contemporary Strategy Analysis*, Third Edition, 1998, Blackwell, p. 461.

Günther, T., 'Value-based performance measures for decentral organisational units', Dresden University. Paper presented at the *European Accounting Association Meeting* in Graz, 1997, p. 24.

Günther, T., Landrock, B., and Muche, T. (1999) 'Profit versus value based performance measures', Dresden University. Working paper as yet unpublished, 27 pp.

Haspeslagh, P., Noda, T., and Boulos, F. (2001) 'Managing for value: It's not just about the numbers', *Harvard Business Review*, July/August, 2001, 62–74.

Hillman, A. J., and Keim, G. D., 'Shareholder value, stakeholder management, and social issues: what's the bottom line?', *Strategic Management Journal*, Vol. 22, 2001, 125–139.

Institute of Management Accountants, 'Measuring and managing shareholder value creation', Statement No. 4AA, 31 March, 1997, Institute of Management Accountants.

Ittner, C. D., and Larcker, D. F., 'Are nonfinancial measures leading indicators of financial performance? An analysis of customer satisfaction'. *Journal of Accounting Research*, Vol. 36, 1998, 1–35.

Kenney, C., 'Buying trouble: Avoiding the acquisition pitfalls', *Shareholder Value Added*, Vol. XIX, 8 pp. (www.lek.com).

Kenney, C., 'Creating an ownership-oriented culture', *Shareholder Value Added*, Vol. II, 8 pp. (www.lek.com).

Kenney, C., 'Market signals analysis: A vital tool for managing market expectations', *Shareholder Value Added*, Vol. IX, 8 pp. (www.lek.com).

Kissel, M., 'A passion for value', *Marakon Commentary*, Marakon Associates, Vol. IV, Issue 3, March 1998, 8 pp.

Koller, T., 'What is value-based management?', *McKinsey Quarterly*, No. 3, 1994, 87–101.

Kontes, P., 'Strategy happens', *Marakon Commentrary*, Marakon Associates, Vol. IV, Issue 1, March 1998, 8 pp.

Kotter, J. P., 'Leading change: Why transformation efforts fail', *Harvard Business Reveiw*, March/April, 1995, 59–67.

Kozin, M., 'Using shareholder value analysis for acquisitions', *Shareholder Value Added*, Vol. III, 8 pp. (www.lek.com).

KPMG Consulting, *Value-Based Management – The Growing Importance of Shareholder Value in Europe*, 1999, p. 20.

Leahy, T., 'Making their mark', *Business of Finance*, June, 2000.

Lehn, K., and Makhija, A. K., 'EVA and MVA as performance measures and signals for strategic change', *Strategy & Leadership*, May/June, 1996, 34–38.

Lehn, K., and Makhija, A. K., 'EVA, accounting profits and CEO turnover: An empirical examination 1985–1994', *Journal of Applied Corporate Finance*, Vol. 10, No. 2, Summer, 1997, 90–97.

Madden, B. J., 'The CFROI valuation model', *Journal of Investing*, Spring, 1998, 31–43.

Madden, B. J., *CFROI Valuation (Cash Flow Return On Investment)*, a Total System Approach to Valuing the Firm, Great Britain, 1999, Butterworth–Heinemann Finance, 352 pp.

Marsh, D. G., 'Making or breaking value', *New Zealand Management*, March, 1999, 58–59.

Martin, J. D., and Petty, J. W., *Value-Based Management – the Corporate Response to the Shareholder Revolution*, 2000, Harvard Business School Press, 249 pp.

McLaren, J., 'A strategic perspective on economic value added', *Management Accounting*, April, 1999, 30–32.

McLaren, J., 'EVA[R] – for planning and control: some preliminary evidence from New Zealand', *BAA Annual Conference*, held at Exeter, UK, April, 2000, 32 pp.

McTaggart, J., and Gillis, S., 'Setting targets to maximise shareholder value', *Strategy & Leadership*, Vol. 26, Issue 2, March/April, 1998, 18–21.

McTaggart, J., and Kontes, P. W., 'The governing corporate objective: Shareholders versus stakeholders', *Marakon Commentary*, Marakon Associates, June, 1993, p. 26.

McTaggart, J. M., Kontes, P. W., and Mankins, M., *The Value Imperative*, 1994, The Free Press, 367 pp.

Merchant, K. A., *Modern Management Control Systems Text and Cases*, 1998, Prentice Hall, 851 pp.

Miller, K., 'The business of knowing', *Information World Review*, April, 2000, 22–23.

Mills, R., and Print, C., 'Strategic value analysis', *Management Accounting*, February, 1995, 35–37.

Mills, R., and Weinstein, B., 'Beyond shareholder value – reconciling the shareholder and stakeholder perspectives', *Journal of General Management*, Vol. 25, No. 3, Spring, 2000, 79–93.

Mills, R., Rowbotham, S., and Robertson, J., 'Using economic profit in assessing business performance', *Management Accounting UK*, November, 1998, 34–38.

Minchington, C., and Francis, G., 'Divisional performance measures: EVA – as a proxy for shareholder wealth', *International Journal Business Performance Management*, Vol. 2, Nos 1–3, 98–107, 2000.

Morin, R. A., and Jarrell, S. L., *Driving Shareholder Value – Value-Building Techniques for Creating Shareholder Wealth*, 2001, McGraw-Hill, 399 pp.

Myers, R., 'Metric wars – marketing battles erupt as Stern Stewart and rivals seek your hearts, minds and dollars', *CFO*, October, 1996, 41–50.

Nodine, T., 'Making real decisions with real options', *Shareholder Value Added*, Vol. XVI, 8 pp. (www.lek.com).

O'Byrne, S. F., 'EVA® and market value', *Journal of Applied Corporate Finance*, Vol. 9, No. 1, Spring, 1996, 16–25.

O'Hanlon, J., and Peasnell, K. (1998) 'Wall Street's contribution to management accounting: The "Stern Stewart EVA" financial management system', *Management Accounting Research*, Vol. 9, 1998, 421–444.

O'Hanlon, J., and Peasnell, K., *Residual Income and Value Creation: The Missing Link*, 19 March, 2001, Lancaster University, Department of Accounting and Finance, pp. 34 pp.

Ottosen, E., and Weissenrieder, F., 'Cash value added – a framework for value-based management', *Ekonomi & Styrning, Sweden*, May, 1996 (www.anelda.com).

Plender, J., 'Giving people a stake in the future', *Long Range Planning*, Vol. 31, No. 2, 1998, 211–217.

Pratt, S. P., *Cost of Capital, Estimation and Applications, United States of America*, 1998, John Wiley & Sons, 226 pp.

PricewaterhouseCoopers, *Inside the Mind of the CEO in Belgium*, 2000, 24 pp.

Pruzan, P., 'From control to value-based management and accountability', *Journal of Business Ethics*, No. 17, 1998, 1379–1394.

Rappaport, A., 'Executive incentives vs. corporate growth', *Harvard Business Review*, July/August, 1978, 81–87.

Rappaport, A., 'Strategic analysis for more profitable acquisitions', *Harvard Business Review*, July/August, 1979, 99–109.

Rappaport, A., 'Selecting strategies that create shareholder value', *Harvard Business Review*, May/June, 1981, 139–149.

Rappaport, A., *Creating Shareholder Value*, 1986, The Free Press, p. 270.

Rappaport, A., 'Stock market signals to managers', *Harvard Business Review*, November/December, 1987, 57–62.

Rappaport, A., 'The staying power of the public corporation', *Harvard Business Review*, January/February, 1990, 2–9.

Rappaport, A., 'CFO and strategists: Forging a common framework', *Harvard Business Review*, May/June, 1992, 84–90.

Rappaport, A., *Creating Shareholder Value*, 1998, The Free Press, p. 205.

Rappaport, A., 'New thinking on how to link executive pay with performance', *Harvard Business Review*, March/April, 1999, 91–101.

Rappaport, A., and Mauboussin, M., 'Using expectations investing to develop and communicate strategy', *Shareholder Value Added*, Vol. XVIII, 8 pp. (www.lek.com).

Rappaport, A., 'Excerpts from creating shareholder value: A guide for managers and investors', *Shareholder Value Added*, Vol. V, 8.

Read, C., *CFO Architect of the Corporation's Future*, United States of America, 1997, John Wiley & Sons, p. 300.

Reimann, B. C., *Managing for Value: a Guide to Value-Based Strategic Management*, 1987, The Planning Forum, 247 pp.

Reimann, B. C., 'Shareholder value and executive compensation', *Planning Review*, May/June, 1991, 41–48.

Rhoads, D., and Goulding, P., 'Successful strategic planning processes', *Shareholder Value Added*, Vol. XVII, 8 pp. (www.lek.com).

Rhoads, D., 'Managing for superior total shareholder returns', *Shareholder Value Added*, Vol. X, 8. (www.lek.com).

Roath, R., 'CFO perspectives: Shareholder value added', *Shareholder Value Added*, Vol. IV, 8. (www.lek.com).

Ronte, H. (1998) 'Value-based management', *Management Accounting*, January, 38.

Schor, L., 'Identifying and managing key value drivers', *Shareholder Value Added*, Vol. I, 6 pp. (www.lek.com).

Shankman, N. A., 'Reframing the debate between agency and stakeholder theories of the firm', *Journal of Business Ethics*, No. 19, 1999, 319–334.

Simms, J., 'Marketing for value', *Marketing*, 28 June, 2001, 34–35.

Slater, S. F., and Olson, E. M., 'A value-based management system', *Business Horizons*, September/October, 1996, 48–52.

Smith, C., 'Optimizing price to build shareholder value', *Shareholder Value Added*, Vol. XII, 8 pp. (www.lek.com).

Smith, L. J., 'Consultants battle for SAM (Share of Acronym Market)', *Best's Review*, April, 1997, 43.

Smith, P., 'Shareholder value implementation: Turning promise into reality, *Shareholder Value Added*, Vol. XIV, 8 pp. (www.lek.com).

Stainer, A., and Stainer, L. (1998) 'Business performance – a stakeholder approach', *International Journal of Business Performance Management*, Vol. 1, No. 1, 1998, 2–12.

Stern Stewart, 'ABC, The Balanced Scorecard and EVA®', *EVAluation*, Vol. 1, Issue 2, April, 1999, 5 pp.

Stern, J. M., Shiely, J. S., and Ross, I., *The EVA® Challenge Implementing Value-Added Change in an Organization, United States of America*, 2001, John Wiley & Sons, p. 240.

Stewart, G. B., *The Quest for Value*, 1999, Harper Business, p. 781.

Stewart, T. A., 'Marakon runners', *Fortune*, 28 September, 1998, 153–154.

Yook, K. C., and McCabe, G. M., 'MVA and the cross-section of expected stock returns', *Journal of Portfolio Management*, Spring, 2001, 75–87.

Young, D. S., and O'Byrne, S. F., *EVA® and Value Based Management, A Practical Guide to Implementation*, 2001, McGraw-Hill, p. 493.

Index

acquisitions 80, 122–4, 143–4
Adjusted Present Value method (APV)
    19–23
advertising 43, 45
agency theory 89
Amazon.com 35–6, 49–54
Amoels, A. 87–150
American call options 69
Amram, M. 30
Anthony, R. 142
AOL 35, 43–8
APT *see* Arbitrage Pricing Theory
APV *see* Adjusted Present Value
    method
Arbitrage Pricing Theory (APT) 16
Aristotle 66
Asian crisis 59, 61
asset beta values 13
    see also beta values

banks 18, 38, 41
belief systems 111
benchmarks 139–40
beta values 12–16, 45
biotechnology companies 22, 30
Black, A. 120
bonus bank concept 131–2, 134
bottom-up processes 117
Boulos, F. 103–4
Bromwich, M. 93
Bruggeman, W. 87–150
business units
    collaboration 124

implementation teams 138
performance management 126
resources 121
SBUs 117–18
strategy deployment 116–18

call options
    American calls 69
    equity 31
    option theory 5
    real options 23–4
    start-ups 30
cancellable operating leases 70–72
Capital Asset Pricing Model (CAPM)
    12–14
capital expenditures, real options
    78–80
capital productivity graph, AOL 45
CAPM *see* Capital Asset Pricing Model
cash flow return on investment
    (CFROI) 122
    benchmarks 139
    decision making 122
    metrics 100–2, 141
    residual income theory 101
    reward systems 130
    strategy deployment 119–20
cash flows 8–32, 36–53
    see also discounted cash flow
    benchmarks 139–40
    metrics 142–3
    strategic valuation 3–4
cash value added (CVA), CFROI 101–2

CEOs *see* chief executive officers
CFOs *see* chief financial officers
CFROI *see* cash flow return on
    investment
Chevron 59–60
chief executive officers (CEOs) 104,
    117, 137
chief financial officers (CFOs) 137
coal leases 69–70
Coca-Cola 59, 60–2
collaboration issues 124, 144
commitment issues 103, 111–12
commodity chemicals 75
communications 111–14, 136–7
competitive advantage 114–15
complexity 32, 101
compound options 75, 77–8
consulting companies 105–45
continuing value
    Amazon.com 53, 55
    AOL 46–7, 48
    discounted cash flows 37–8
contracts 132
control processes 87–145
Copeland, T.E. 25, 35–85, 117, 126
corporate valuation 7–33
costs 11–16, 99
    see also weighted average cost of
        capital
cultures 142–3
CVA *see* cash value added

DCF *see* discounted cash flows
De Maeseneire, W. 7–34
decentralisation 138
decision-making
    collaboration 124
    compound rainbow options 78
    decision trees 21–32, 77
    investments 120–2
    multiphased investments 75, 78
    project analysis 80–5
    strategy deployment 115–18
decision-tree analysis (DTA) 21–32
'deep in-the-money' projects 67
deferral options 69–70

development, natural resources 75,
    77–8
differentiation, reward systems 132–3
discounted cash flow (DCF) 36–53
    benchmarks 139–40
    corporate valuation 8–23
    decision-tree analysis 23–6
    enterprise DCF 17–18, 120
    equity DCF 17–18
    extended DCF rule 23
    historical aspects 36
    investments 121–2, 143
    metrics 120, 141
    NPV 36
    real options examples 26–32
    strategic valuation 4
    SVA 142
    volatility issues 22–3
discounted indexed options 135
drivers *see* value drivers
DTA *see* decision-tree analysis

economic profit (EP) 74, 98–9, 120
economic value added (EVA)
    acquisitions/mergers 122
    benchmarks 139–40
    collaboration 124
    communications 113
    equity spreads 100
    expectations-based management
        56–7, 63–4
    implementation teams 137
    investments 121–2
    metrics 98–9, 119–22, 141
    personal computer assembly
        businesses 72, 75
    reward systems 129
    strategic issues 3, 116
    target setting 127
    training 135–6
    WACC 16–17
education 103–4, 135–7, 144–5
empirical tests 38–43, 63
empowerment 103
enterprise discounted cash flow 17–18,
    120

EP *see* economic profit
equity issues 11–16
   see also weighted average cost of
     capital
   beta values 13
   call options 31
   discounted cash flow 17–18
   equity spreads 99–100, 120, 141
EVA *see* economic value added
exercise prices 66
exit decisions 72–5
expansion options 24
expectations-based management
   53–65, 134
exploration, natural resources 75, 77–8
extended discounted cash flow rule 23
external communications 112–13

FCF *see* future free cash flows
financial options 23–4
Five Forces Model (Porter) 115–16
flexibility 67, 81
free cash flows 3–4, 9–11
future free cash flows (FCF) 3–4, 9–11

gain-sharing programmes 104
goldmines 27–8
Gordon model 100
Govindarajan, V. 142
grey box example, real options 68–9
growth issues 11, 38, 42, 92

HOLT Value Associates 100–1, 105–40
hurdle rates 121–2

implementation issues 137–8, 145
indexed options 135
Industry Structure Analysis *see* Five
   Forces Model
INSEAD surveys 96, 98, 102–4
insurance companies 38, 41
interconnections, Metcalf's Law 46–8
internal communications 113–14
Internet companies 22, 84
Internet service providers 43–8

investments 5–6, 76–9, 100–2, 119–22,
   130, 139, 141, 143
Italian companies 38, 40
iterative target setting 28, 128

Japanese companies 38, 40
jet engine manufacturers 71–3

Keenan, A. 25
Kenney, C. 125
Keuleneer, L. 1–6, 7–34
key performance indicators (KPIs) 117,
   126
Koller, T. 37
Kotter, J.P. 93
KPIs *see* key performance indicators
Kulatilaka, N. 30

L.E.K. Consulting 105–40
large companies 39
levered beta values 13
levering concepts 13–14
liquidity 15
listed perspectives 95–7, 141

McKinsey & Co. 105–40
Madden, B.J. 112–13, 119
management 87–145
Marakon Associates 100, 105–40
market issues
   expectations analysis 134
   market to book ratios 48–9, 100, 141
   MVA 96–8, 119, 141
   signals analysis 113, 122–3
market value added (MVA) 96–8, 119,
   141
Markowitz, H. 12
mathematics, real options 68–9
maximisation, shareholder value
   106–7, 128, 140–2
mergers 81, 122–4, 143–4
Metcalf's Law 46–8
metrics
   consulting companies 119–20, 141–3
   multi-period metrics 100–2
   performance 53–6, 92–102, 141–3

metrics (*cont.*)
single period metrics 98–100
SVA 119–20
traditional measures 92–3
value creation 107
value drivers 120
value-based management 95–102
Microsoft 36, 48
mindsets 135–7, 144
mines 27–8
Monte Carlo techniques 37, 81–2
multi-period metrics 100–2
multiphase investments 75–6, 78
Murrin, J. 37
MVA *see* market value added

natural resources, real options 75, 77–8
net present value (NPV) 5–6
discounted cash flows 36
personal computer assembly
businesses 72, 75
project analysis 80
real options 67–8
Noble, C. 37
not-listed perspectives 95, 97–102, 141
NPV *see* net present value

oil companies 75, 77–8
Olson, E.M. 104
operating issues
Amazon.com 53, 55
AOL 44–5
cash flows 3
value-based management 93
options
American calls 69
calls 5, 23–4, 30–1, 70
compound options 77–8
compound rainbow options 75, 77–8
deferral options 69–70
discounted indexed options 135
financial options 23–4
real options 21–32, 37, 64–81
stock options 134–5
switching options 72–4, 78
theory 4–6

Ottoson, E. 93
ownership issues 103, 125, 129–31

passenger revenue miles 70, 72
payout policies 132–3
performance issues
contracts 132
KPIs 117, 126
management 125–40, 144
metrics 53–6, 92–102, 141–3
reward systems 132–3
personal computer assembly
businesses 72, 75
pharmaceutical companies 21, 30
planning aspects 116–18, 123
plant construction industry 75, 80
Porter, M. 115–16
practical valuation 35–85
price earnings ratio 49, 50, 100, 141
PricewaterhouseCoopers 105–40
projection periods, operating FCFs
10–11
projects 67, 80–5

R&D *see* research and development
rainbow options 75, 77–8
Rappaport, A. 37, 94, 115–18, 123–36,
142
Reader's Digest 51
real options (RO) 21–32, 37, 64–81
reforms 104
regression analysis, TSR 63
relative performance, reward systems
132–3
relevering concepts 14
research and development (R&D) 22,
28–30
residual income theory
CFROI 101
growth 92
metrics 90, 97, 141
resources 120–2
return on assets (ROA) 74, 79
return on invested capital (ROIC) 17,
64
reward systems 128–35, 144

risks 12–16, 37, 78, 81, 84–5
RO *see* real options
ROA *see* return on assets
robust growth companies 38, 42
ROIC *see* return on invested capital

SBUs *see* Strategic Business Units
scarcity 140–1
scenario plans 116
Scheipers, G. 87–150
Sears 57–9
SFP *see* Small Firm Premium
share sensitivity analysis 53
The Shareholder Scoreboard (L.E.K.
    Consulting) 112
shareholder value
    consulting companies 112
    maximisation 106–7, 128, 140–2
    stakeholders 93–4, 140
    strategic issues 2–4, 118
    training 137
    TSR 57–63, 95–6, 141
    value-based management 90–2, 140
shareholder value added (SVA)
    DCF 142
    metrics 119–20
    reward systems 134
    value drivers 102
shareholder value analysis (SVA) 3–4
signals analysis 113, 122–3
single period metrics 98–100
Slater, S.F. 104
Small Firm Premium (SFP) 15–16
Smith, P. 117, 130, 136
'socially responsible business
    behaviour' 94
spreadsheets 36–7
stakeholders 93–4, 140
    see also shareholder value
start-ups 30–1
Stern Stewart and Co. 105–40
Stewart, G.B. 98–9, 113
stock options 134–5
stock splits 50–1, 54
Strategic Business Units (SBUs) 117–18
strategic issues 1–6

deployment 116–19
development 114–16
management 143
resources 121
reward systems 131–3
value creations 107
striking prices *see* exercise prices
structures, management 142
success factors 104
superior performances 129
surveys 96, 98, 102–4, 136–7
SVA *see* shareholder value added;
    shareholder value analysis
switching options 72–4, 78
systems management 142–3

t-tests 63
target setting 126–8, 144
taxes 20
teams 137–8, 145
tests 38–43, 63
Thales 66–7
time issues 134
top management 129–30, 137–8, 145
top-down approaches 117
total shareholder return (TSR) 57–63,
    95–6, 141
traditional performance measures
    53–6, 92–3
training 103–4, 135–7, 144–5
transaction maps 123–4
transformation teams 138
TSR *see* total shareholder return

uncertainty 37, 78, 81, 84–5
unlevering concepts 14

*Valuation: Measuring and Managing
    the Value of Companies* (Cope-
    land, Koller, Murrin) 35, 37
value
    analysis 3–4
    maximisation 106–7, 128, 140–2
    transformation teams 138
value creation
    consulting companies 107

value creation (*cont.*)
    reward systems 129, 132
    stakeholders 94
    strategic valuation 2–4
    traditional measures 93
value drivers
    collaboration 124
    metrics 120
    performance management 125–7
    shareholder value added 102
    strategic issues 4, 118–20
value-based management (VBM) 2–4,
    87–145
Verhoog, W. 1–6
vision 2
volatility
    discounted cash flows 22–3
    project analysis 82
    real options 31

risks 12–16
uncertainty 37, 78, 81, 84–5

WACC *see* weighted average cost of
    capital
waiting, real options 26–7
Wal-Mart 56–9
Walker, D. 130
websites 18
weighted average cost of capital
    (WACC)
    Adjusted Present Value method 20–1
    Amazon.com 54
    AOL 45–6, 48
    corporate valuation 9, 11–16
    economic value added 16–17
    expectations-based management 64
    strategic valuation 3–4
Weissenrieder, F. 93